CW01468497

To:

_____

From:

_____

A HEARTBEAT
of
HOPE

CHRISTIAN ART
PUBLISHERS

Published by Christian Art Publishers
PO Box 1599, Vereeniging, 1930

© 2004
First edition 2004
Second edition 2020

Devotions written by Nina Smit

Cover designed by Christian Art Publishers

Designed by Christian Art Publishers

Images used under license from Shutterstock.com

Unless otherwise indicated Scripture quotations are taken from
the *Holy Bible*, New International Version®. NIV®. Copyright © 1973,
1978, 1984 by International Bible Society. Used by permission of
Zondervan Publishing House. All rights reserved.

Scripture quotations from THE MESSAGE.
Copyright © by Eugene H. Peterson 1993, 1994, 1995.
Used by permission of NavPress Publishing Group.

Set in 13 on 16 pt Cronos Pro by Christian Art Publishers

Printed in China

ISBN 978-1-4321-3122-7

© All rights reserved. No part of this book may be reproduced in
any form without permission in writing from the publisher,
except in the case of brief quotations in critical articles or reviews.

20 21 22 23 24 25 26 27 28 29 – 10 9 8 7 6 5 4 3 2 1

January

A BRAND NEW YEAR

The LORD himself goes before you and will be with
you; he will never leave you nor forsake you.
Do not be afraid; do not be discouraged.

DEUTERONOMY 31:8

*T*oday is the first day of a brand new year! You can enter this year with confidence and joy, knowing that God is with you. He promises to go before you and make a way for you. You have His assurance that He will never leave you nor forsake you.

You don't need to be anxious or afraid as you face an unknown future because God loves you and holds your future in His hands.

Father, thank You for Your assurance that You will never leave me nor forsake me. No matter what challenges I may face, I can confidently move forward knowing that You are always with me. Amen.

THE RIGHT ROAD

Let the morning bring me word of your unfailing love, for I have put my trust in you. Show me the way I should go, for to you I lift up my soul.

PSALM 143:8

The psalmist prays that God will show him the way he should go. He puts his hope in God because he knows that God has prepared a future in heaven for all His children.

At the beginning of a new year we all hope that our year will be pleasant and problem-free. This year, place your hope in God alone and you will become aware of His wonders around you in a new way every day. Stay close to Him, and He will direct you along the right paths.

He loves you and cares about what happens to you.

Lord, I know that this year will come with its own set of struggles. That is why I place my hope in You. You alone can guide me along the right path. *Amen.*

GOD IS FAITHFUL
TO HIS PROMISES

Let us hold unswervingly to the hope we profess,
for he who promised is faithful.

HEBREWS 10:23

God is absolutely faithful to each one of His promises. When we trust in Him we don't need to fear because we have the confident assurance that He does what He says He will do.

Even when it seems at times that one of these promises is not being fulfilled in your life, you should still keep trusting. Keep hoping in God. He is faithful. He will fulfill each one of His promises for your life at exactly the right time. Trust Him for that!

Father, because of Your faithfulness I never have to feel hopeless. Thank You for being the steadfast rock I can trust.

Amen.

THANK YOU!

Jesus asked, "Were not all ten cleansed?
Where are the other nine?"

LUKE 17:17

Of the ten lepers whom Jesus healed, only one came back to thank Him. Many people live lives of ingratitude. We are all eager to ask God for things and then when we receive them, we so easily forget to thank Him.

Make living with gratitude in your heart one of your resolutions this year. Try not to take the blessings of God for granted. Make an effort to thank God each day for one thing that you have never thanked Him for before.

You will discover that your life is filled with abundant, joy-filled blessings.

Father, I never want to take Your blessings for granted. Give me a heart of gratitude and praise for all You've done for me.

Amen.

MAKE THE MOST
OF EACH DAY

This is the day the LORD has made;
let us rejoice and be glad in it.

PSALM 118:24

Each new day is a gift straight from the hand of God – a gift guaranteed to give you joy and make you happy.

There are still 361 days to use and enjoy this year. Make the most of each day – today only comes once, and once it has past, you can never get it back again. Use every opportunity that comes your way, and rejoice in every new day because God has made it especially for you!

Help me to make the best of every new day, Lord, rejoicing in Your goodness towards me. Amen.

THE GIFT OF LIFE

You make known to me the path of life;
you will fill me with joy in your presence,
with eternal pleasures at your right hand.

PSALM 16:11

It is wonderful to be alive. To taste God's grace and goodness each day. To love others and to be loved by others and God. We should never become blasé about the wonders of life.

Life is a gift from the hand of God and you can enjoy it abundantly every day. He wants your year to be filled with joy and gladness and He wants you to delight in the people whom you love every day.

Lord, I delight in every joy-filled moment, every blessing of grace and love You've given me. Thank You. Amen.

GOD WILL LEAD YOU

*If you spend yourselves in behalf of the hungry
and satisfy the needs of the oppressed, then
your light will rise in the darkness, and your
night will become like the noonday.*

ISAIAH 58:10

*O*ur Father meets our needs and comes to help others in their need. When you help the needy and oppressed your light shines in the darkness and God is glorified.

Make a decision right now to be sensitive to the needs of others. Ask the Lord to open your eyes and ears to other people, and do not put off doing something practical to help those who need it. Then you will live in His light this year.

Father, give me a heart for others. Open my eyes to their needs and how I can help them. Amen.

THE LORD WILL BE YOUR HELP

If the LORD delights in a man's way,
he makes his steps firm.

PSALM 37:23

*T*he Lord wants to guide you and support and help you in everything that you undertake this year. He wants to reveal to you how He wants you to live. He wants to direct your path.

The promise in this verse comes with a condition: God will support and guide you as long as you live according to His ways. Live each day in such a way that God will be pleased with the things you do and say.

Lord, help me to live every day according to Your will and not my own. Guide me in the way everlasting. Amen.

PUT YOUR HOPE IN GOD

O Lord, be gracious to us; we long for you.
Be our strength every morning,
our salvation in time of distress.

ISAIAH 33:2

*T*he people of God turned to Him for help every time things went terribly wrong for them. And He was always willing to respond to their cries.

In the unknown year that lies before you, you can confidently place your hope in God each day: He is still a refuge for His children in times of trouble. He will help you and strengthen you, as He has always done for His beloved children.

God, I turn to You for refuge and strength. You are my hope and my help. Amen.

GOD IS ALWAYS NEAR

Your name, O LORD, endures forever, your renown,
O LORD, through all generations.

PSALM 135:13

*G*od is eternal and unchanging. He proves His support and trustworthy love from one generation to another to those who love Him and serve Him. Even though we may sometimes be unfaithful to Him, He remains faithful to us.

There is one fact that you can carry with you through this year: God is with you. He will never forsake you. When you have need of Him, you can call on Him – He will never disappoint you.

Thank You, Lord, that no matter what I do, You remain faith-ful and steadfast in Your love for me. Amen.

January 11

GOD'S WAY

*Although the Lord gives you the bread of adversity
and the water of affliction ... Whether you turn to
the right or to the left, your ears will hear a voice
behind you, saying, "This is the way; walk in it."*

ISAIAH 30:20-21

$\mathcal{P}$arents love their children but discipline them when
they are disobedient. In the same way, God sometimes
allows troubling times to come to those of His children
who stray from the right road. In this manner He lovingly
brings them back to Him.

If you wander away from God, He might allow you
to go through difficulties so that you will learn to know
His will. Remember that crises in your life are often God's
way of drawing you closer to Him – take the opportunity
to learn from them.

*Father, help me to learn from the difficulties I face, always
drawing closer to You. Amen.*

January 12

THE LOVE OF JESUS

So that you may be able to discern what is best and
may be pure and blameless until the day of Christ,
filled with the fruit of righteousness that comes
through Jesus Christ – to the glory and praise of God.

PHILIPPIANS 1:10-11

The love of Jesus will change your life forever because it changes your priorities and brings you into a right relationship with God.

Therefore, the closer you live to Jesus, the more others will see how wonderful God is through all that you do. Make your resolution this year to be led by the love of Jesus and to become more and more like Him.

Jesus, help me to become more and more like You, following Your example of love. Amen.

LOVE MEANS …

*And this is my prayer: that your love may abound
more and more in knowledge and depth of insight,
so that you may be able to discern what is best and
may be pure and blameless until the day of Christ.*

PHILIPPIANS 1:9-10

*I*f Jesus' love is in your life, you will be able to understand other people better. The love of Jesus compels you to care for other people and it creates in you a sensitivity for the needs of others.

Live close to Jesus. Ask Him to cause His love to grow in you day by day this year so that your understanding and compassion will increase and you will make the right decisions and choices.

*Lord Jesus, let Your love grow in me more and more each day,
allowing me to see others the way You see them. Amen.*

LOVE AND PRAYERS

"But I tell you: Love your enemies and pray for those who persecute you."

MATTHEW 5:44

*I*t is easy to pray for the people you love. But it is a completely different thing to pray for those who stand in your way, who outshine you in various areas, those who do their best to belittle you. And yet Jesus expects this of you.

The people who least deserve your love and prayers usually need it the most. Set aside a special time each day this year to pray for them.

Lord, help me to pray for those who belittle me, discourage me and treat me unfairly. They too deserve Your love, forgiveness and hand of blessing in their lives. Amen.

NEVER ALONE

*Praise be to the L*ORD*, to God our Savior,*
who daily bears our burdens.

PSALM 68:19

*A*s a Christian, you need never feel alone. God is with you every day. And because God is with you, you have the assurance that He will help and support you. You know that God will carry you when you feel you cannot take another step.

God undertakes to give you enough strength for each day. If things become too hard for you this year, you can lean on God's strength moment by moment.

God our Savior, I lean on Your strength to help me through the difficult times. Please carry me when I can no longer walk.

Amen.

THE LOVE OF JESUS ENVELOPS YOU

I pray that you may grasp how wide and long and high and deep is the love of Christ, and to know this love that surpasses knowledge.

EPHESIANS 3:17-19

*J*esus' love for you is so all-embracing that it fills every area of your life to overflowing. We cannot find the words to describe His love. We cannot understand how a holy God can have so much love for unworthy sinners. But we can accept this love for ourselves.

The closer you live to God this year, the more the love He demonstrated in Jesus Christ will become a reality in your life.

Thank You, Lord Jesus, for Your all-embracing love and care for me. Amen.

GOD OFFERS PEACE

My heart is not proud, O LORD, my eyes are not haughty; I do not concern myself with great matters or things too wonderful for me. But I have stilled and quieted my soul; like a weaned child with its mother, like a weaned child is my soul within me.

PSALM 131:1-2

There isn't a more beautiful picture of absolute contentment than that of a baby asleep in her mother's arms. God wants to give you the same kind of complete contentment this year.

God offers you His peace in exchange for your anxiety. If you are willing to wait for Him, He will cause His rest and peace to permeate your life. You can leave your worries and concerns with Him. Will you accept this offer of His?

Lord, I bring my worries and lay them at Your feet. Patiently I will wait for Your perfect rest and peace. Amen.

January 18

ABSOLUTE SURRENDER

May God himself, the God of peace, sanctify you
through and through. May your whole spirit,
soul and body be kept blameless at
the coming of our Lord Jesus Christ.

1 THESSALONIANS 5:23

*T*he secret of inner peace is absolute surrender to God. Surrender means that you willingly give your whole life to God. It means to do only what He wants you to do and to put Him first in all things. Surrender means to submit your will to His in all things.

If you yield everything to Him, you will live each day in the shelter of His love this year.

I surrender my life to You, Lord. Help me to obey Your will so that I might experience Your perfect peace. Amen.

January 19

YOU CAN BE COURAGEOUS

"I have told you these things, so that in me you may have peace. In this world you will have trouble. But take heart! I have overcome the world."

JOHN 16:33

*T*his year is bound to have a few challenges and possible hurdles. Sometimes it feels as if all the negative things we face in life knock us off course.

If you are feeling desperate today, Jesus' message is meant especially for you: although you can expect to encounter difficulties, it is still possible to keep your head above water because Jesus has overcome the world. With His power at your disposal, you too will be an overcomer this year!

Lord Jesus, because of You, I can overcome any difficulty. Thank You. Amen.

DEPENDENT ON GOD

We were under great pressure, far beyond our
ability to endure, so that we despaired even of life … But
this happened that we might not rely on ourselves
but on God, who raises the dead.

2 CORINTHIANS 1:8-9

*W*hen everything in life is going well, we sometimes imagine that we can get by without God. If our bank account is healthy, we don't see the need for praying for our daily bread.

But life has a way of knocking us off our feet. That is when we realize that difficult times are actually beneficial because they teach us exactly how much we do need to depend on God. Remember this next time a crisis erupts in your life.

Father, I am grateful that the difficulties I face help to draw me closer to You. Amen.

LOOK THROUGH HIS EYES

*For we are God's workmanship, created in
Christ Jesus to do good works, which God
prepared in advance for us to do.*

EPHESIANS 2:10

You are the work of God's hands. And you are exceedingly wonderfully made. He created you for good works – and you will only truly understand His purpose for your life when you look at the world through His eyes.

Make an effort to make a positive difference in the lives of the people and the world around you this year. Live in such a way that the world will be a better place because you were prepared to do the good things that God has planned for you to do.

Lord, show me Your purpose for my life. Help me to be Your light in a dark world. Amen.

LIVE YOUR FAITH

As the body without the spirit is dead,
so faith without deeds is dead.

JAMES 2:26

*I*t is essential for Christians to be obedient to God, to do the things that He asks of them. It doesn't help to tell people that we believe in Christ if our lifestyle contradicts our words. If that is so, then James declares that we are actually dead.

If you believe in Christ, your faith should be evident in everything you say, do and think. Let your faith shine through your words and behavior towards others. Make a decision right now to live like a child of God this year.

Father, let my faith be evident in every area of my life.

Amen.

TRUE FAITH

Do not say to your neighbor, "Come back later;
I'll give it tomorrow" – when you now have it with you.

PROVERBS 3:28

*T*rue faith requires that you take note of the needs of the people around you and do something tangible to help them. If you do not help and love the people whom you can see, it is not possible for you to love God whom you cannot see, John writes in 1 John 4:20.

Let your love for God be evident in your actions. This year, show how much you love God by reaching out to other people, and helping them – without delay!

Lord, I love You so much. Help me to show my love for You by the way I live. Amen.

GOD KNOWS

Does he not see my ways and count my every step?

JOB 31:4

God already knows what you will go through this year. He is completely in control of your future.

If you love and serve Him, He promises to be by your side each day, to keep an eye on you at all times, to watch over every step that you take.

It is wonderful to know that the God of the universe cares about each one of us. We never have to walk alone.

Lord God, I give all my cares and worries to You. You hold the future in Your hands that is why I hope in You. *Amen.*

PEACE IN YOUR LIFE

Let the peace of Christ rule in your hearts,
since as members of one body you were
called to peace. And be thankful.

COLOSSIANS 3:15

We all want peace in our lives. But in the world around us, and even in our own lives, we see very little of God's peace. Instead of the peace that Christ gives, we are surrounded by violence and unrest.

Yet it is possible to live in peace with God and with others. If you allow God to be the referee over the conflicts in your life this year, and if you accept His decisions, you will experience His peace in your life.

Father God, help me to be an instrument of Your peace, following Your will and not my own. Amen.

ANCHOR YOUR FAITH
IN JESUS CHRIST

Such is the destiny of all who forget God; so perishes the hope of the godless. What he trusts in is fragile; what he relies on is a spider's web.

JOB 8:13-14

*J*ob was bitter because things were going so badly for him and yet so well for the unbelievers around him. He could not understand God's way of doing things. But when he considered the final outcome of wickedness, a glimmer of understanding broke through: they have no hope for tomorrow.

While unbelievers build their lives on a spider's web of hope, believers are anchored in the Rock of Jesus Christ. If you ever begin to doubt God's goodness toward you, hold fast to the "hope of glory" that God has promised to His children.

Lord, no matter what happens, I will hold fast to the eternal hope I have in You. Amen.

THE INITIATIVE OF LOVE

We love because he first loved us.

1 JOHN 4:19

God's love for us is a gift of grace. And our love for God is also a gift of His grace. Grace means that love always originates with God.

It is only because God first loved us, while we were yet sinners, that the death of Christ on the cross made it possible for us to become His children. And for us to be able to love Him in return.

We are not able to love in our own strength – not God and not other people. It is God who initiates love in the hearts of His children.

God, thank You for Your gift of grace and love. Amen.

HE DIED FOR YOU

But God demonstrates his own love for us in this:
While we were still sinners, Christ died for us.

ROMANS 5:8

*G*od demonstrated His love for us in that He gave His only Son to die in our place, so that, if we believe in Him, we will live forever.

Because Jesus was prepared to die for you while you were still a sinner, He made it possible for you to receive the gift of God's grace. He paid the full price for your sins on the cross. And He now asks you to love each person who crosses your path in life with that same love.

Will you do so?

Jesus, You are an example of true love. Help me to follow Your example and love others the way You love me. Amen.

DON'T DELAY

For he says, "In the time of my favor I heard you, and in the day of salvation I helped you." I tell you, now is the time of God's favor, now is the day of salvation.

2 CORINTHIANS 6:2

God offers His grace to you as a free gift. But His offer of grace can come to an end. None of us knows exactly how long we will live.

Therefore, if you have not yet done so, today is the right time to respond to God's offer of love. Do not let the opportunity slip through your fingers. Accept God's gift of grace today – tomorrow might be too late.

God, I humbly accept Your offer of grace. Fill my heart with Your Spirit and Your love. Amen.

GIVING BRINGS JOY

In everything I did, I showed you that by this kind
of hard work we must help the weak, remembering
the words the Lord Jesus himself said: "It is more blessed
to give than to receive."

ACTS 20:35

*J*esus said that it is more blessed to give than to receive. Those who are prepared to share their possessions with others have already discovered how true it is. Giving definitely brings more joy than receiving. When you give someone a gift and you see her face light up with joy, it thrills your heart too.

God gave His Son to you, and Jesus gave His life for you. What will you give Him?

Father God, You have given me so much. Thank You for blessing me with Your grace and love and kindness. *Amen.*

LEAVE THE BAGGAGE OF THE PAST

One thing I do: Forgetting what is behind and straining toward what is ahead, I press on toward the goal to win the prize for which God has called me heavenward in Christ Jesus.

PHILIPPIANS 3:13-14

*Y*ou might have made a few mistakes in the year that has past. Choose to begin this year without the burden of regret and gird yourself up to reach the finishing line.

Right now, stop stressing about all the things that went wrong in the year that has past. Forget about your mistakes. Make a point to learn from your mistakes and try to never make the same mistakes again. Look forward towards the goal that is ahead of you this year.

Lord, please help me to put my failures and mistakes behind me. Help me to focus on You alone. Amen.

February

JOYFUL DAY

O my Strength, I sing praise to you; you,
O God, are my fortress, my loving God.

PSALM 59:17

A day begun with a song of praise is a day filled with sunshine. How can you go through life and not be aware of the joy it offers if you begin each day by praising God for everything that He does for you and gives to you?

That is why you should try to begin each day with a song of praise. Find something new to praise God for every day. Then each day will be a day on which you are conscious that God Himself is by your side. A day filled with joy begins with a song of joy to God.

Loving God, I praise You with all my might. Nothing can surpass Your wonderful blessing and love towards me. Thank You, Jesus. Amen.

TRUST IN GOD

"Because he loves me," says the Lord, *"I will rescue him; I will protect him, for he acknowledges my name."*

PSALM 91:14

*G*od promises to send His angels to protect His children against dangers. And yet we often hear of Christians who are sick and suffering, Christians who are attacked and killed. How do we reconcile these things with God's promise of protection?

Even though we are not guaranteed freedom from danger in this world, we can still trust God for peace of mind and security every day. God is with you even in dangerous situations, even when you walk through the valley of the shadow of death.

Lord, in the midst of trouble I may not always be able to see Your purpose or plan, but I can rest assured that You are always with me. Amen.

February 3

GOD REWARDS FAITH

*A stone was brought and placed over the
mouth of the den, and the king sealed it ... so
that Daniel's situation might not be changed.*

DANIEL 6:17

When Daniel was taken away into exile and made to work for a heathen king, he still believed in God. Three times a day he prayed to the God whom he loved. And God protected and blessed him, just as He still loves and protects each of His children today.

God rewarded Daniel's faith with a series of miracles – He delivered him out of the lions' den and his friends out of the fiery furnace. God can still perform wonders in your life, if you believe in Him and, as Daniel did, serve Him with all your heart.

God, here I am, ready to serve. Lead me according to Your will and plan for my life. Amen.

GOD LOVES YOU

"For God so loved the world that he gave his one and only Son, that whoever believes in him shall not perish but have eternal life."

JOHN 3:16

*J*ohn 3:16 must be the most well-known verse in the Bible. We learn it by heart when we are just tiny tots. This exceptional verse contains God's declaration of love to the world. God gives each one of us a second chance because of His love for us.

The central message of the Bible can be summarized in this one statement: God loves you so much that He sent His Son to die in your place. To receive the gift of eternal life for yourself, you need to believe in Jesus.

Your love for Your children, for me, Lord, is beyond understanding. I rejoice in Your love and promise of eternal life.

Amen.

LOVE IS A DECISION

Dear friends, let us love one another,
for love comes from God. Everyone who
loves has been born of God and knows God.

1 JOHN 4:7

*O*f all the things that God asks His children to do, this is the most difficult: to love one another. We cannot love one another through our own efforts, let alone love others with the same love with which God loves us! The good news is that we do not have to try to do so. God makes it possible for us to love through His Holy Spirit who lives in us.

Love for God and others is never simply emotion. You can make the decision to love with God's help, and He will help you live out your decision.

Father, give me a heart for Your children. Fill my heart with love for others, even those I don't necessarily like. Help me to see them through Your eyes. Amen.

SERVE OTHER PEOPLE

"The greatest among you will be your servant."

MATTHEW 23:11

*S*erving other people is extremely important to Jesus. He Himself said that the Son of Man did not come to be served but to serve. And if we truly love Him we will want to follow His example: to be of service to others.

Even the most important among us need to be ready and willing to serve others. If you are prepared to serve others here on earth, then you will be rewarded in heaven.

Lord, help me to be the least, to serve others in humility and to live out Your love for all to experience. Amen.

OF ETERNAL VALUE

*Let him not deceive himself by trusting
what is worthless, for he will get nothing in return.*

JOB 15:31

Each of us has certain things to which we attach great value. We are too easily inclined to trust ourselves and our material possessions. But, as Eliphaz pointed out to Job, all our earthly possessions and securities, which seem so important to us, are actually worth nothing.

We should value only those things that have eternal value. Spend your time and energy on things that will last forever. And trust in God alone.

Father God, help me to not attribute so much value to material things, rather help me to focus on the things that have eternal value. Amen.

THE LOVE OF GOD

May your unfailing love rest upon us,
O LORD, even as we put our hope in you.

PSALM 33:22

*T*he psalmist asks God to surround him with His love because his hope is in God alone. He knows that the people of God trusted Him and had experienced His protection time and time again.

Make this your prayer too. God is always worthy of your trust. Trust God and ask Him to cover you with His love. If the banner of God's love has been raised over you, you have no need to fear anything.

Thank You, Father, for covering me with Your love. Because You are with me, I need not fear. Amen.

February 9

TRUST HIM

He will be the sure foundation for your times,
a rich store of salvation and wisdom and knowledge;
the fear of the LORD is the key to this treasure.

ISAIAH 33:6

*T*he prophet Isaiah tells us that God is the only One in whom we can place our trust all through our lives. God has never, since the beginning of time, left one of His children in the lurch.

As a child of God, you can face each new day with joy and peace of mind because you know for certain the God in whom you trust is worthy of your trust. You can depend on Him each day for the rest of your life. You can build your future on His wisdom and knowledge.

Lord, I put my trust in You, knowing that no matter what happens, I can face each day with joy and peace because You are faithful. Amen.

HE LIVES IN YOU

Even though I walk through the valley of the
shadow of death, I will fear no evil, for you are with me;
your rod and your staff, they comfort me.

PSALM 23:4

God is always personally present with each one of His children. He lives in you through His Holy Spirit and your safety is guaranteed in His hands. Therefore, you need never fear.

Even when you walk through times of deep darkness, you need not be fearful at all. Your Shepherd is by your side. He will carry you through the dark valleys. In His hands you are always safe. And on the other side of the darkness of life, He is waiting to welcome you to your eternal home.

You are our Shepherd, Lord. You are with us every step of the way. Because You hold us in Your hands, we do not have to be afraid. Amen.

February 11

HE REJOICES OVER YOU

The LORD your God is with you, he is mighty to save.
He will take great delight in you, he will quiet you with
his love, he will rejoice over you with singing.

ZEPHANIAH 3:17

A woman who suffers from bouts of depression, once nurtured a seed of joy in her heart for the whole day. "It is that verse in Zephaniah that says God delights in me – isn't that fantastic?" she exclaimed in delight, when she shared her joy with friends.

God wants to be your Deliverer. He loves you. He is with you each and every day. But best of all, the God who created the whole world rejoices over you! That is indeed a reason to rejoice!

God, You delight in me. How amazing is that! You know my deepest weaknesses and still You rejoice over every detail of my life. Thank You. Amen.

BE THANKFUL

However many years a man may live, let him
enjoy them all. ... Be happy, young man,
while you are young, and let your heart give
you joy in the days of your youth.

ECCLESIASTES 11:8-9

Very few of God's children truly realize how ungrateful they are. Most of us are so used to being healthy and having enough of everything, that we lose sight of the millions of people in the world who suffer lack, and who are sick and hungry.

Make counting your blessings every day part of your lifestyle. From now on, live each day with gratitude and enthusiasm: make each day a celebration because you belong to God.

Thank You for the abundance of blessings You pour over my life every day, Lord. Help me to never lose sight of all the wonderful blessings I have. Amen.

REMEMBER YOUR RESPONSIBILITIES

Follow the ways of your heart and whatever your eyes see, but know that for all these things God will bring you to judgment.

ECCLESIASTES 11:9

Some people maintain that God is a spoilsport who wants to subject His children to dozens of rules and regulations. Nothing could be further from the truth!

God actually gives His law to us to show us how we can be truly happy. He wants us to be able to do the things that are fun and that we enjoy. There is just one condition: that we will always remember that we also have a responsibility to live holy lives, because God will hold us accountable for the way in which we live.

Father God, help me to never be so busy enjoying my life that I forget about Your commandments and Your will for my life.

Amen.

HOPE IS MEANINGFUL

May the God of hope fill you with all joy and peace as you trust in him, so that you may overflow with hope by the power of the Holy Spirit.

ROMANS 15:13

God is the source of our hope. We know that in the long run He will ensure that everything works out for our best. His Holy Spirit that lives in us makes this hope a reality and at the same time fills us with His joy and peace.

However badly things go for you, you can keep hoping in God. To hope is meaningful – each year spring succeeds the winter, the bright day follows the dark night, and one day, after death, you will be in heaven.

Lord Jesus, I put my hope in You and only You. Amen.

February 15

ETERNAL LIFE

Praise be to the God and Father of our Lord Jesus Christ!
In his great mercy he has given us new birth into
a living hope through the resurrection of Jesus Christ
from the dead, and into an inheritance that can
never perish, spoil or fade – kept in heaven for you.

1 PETER 1:3-4

*C*hristians have an inheritance of incalculable value: the hope which God has in store for us in heaven; a hope that burns brightly, regardless of our present circumstances. It is somewhat ironic that we spend so much time and money on our short earthly life and so little on the life that will last forever.

Make a decision that from today you will give more of your time and energy to your imperishable, pure and eternal inheritance!

Father, help me to put more time and energy into my eternal heritance than I do into things that won't matter in the end.

Amen.

JUST DO IT

Do not withhold good from those who deserve it,
when it is in your power to act.

PROVERBS 3:27

As the proverb rightly says: A stitch in time saves nine. We have all been sorry many times because we have put things off until they eventually deteriorated beyond repair.

You should not put off doing a good deed that would help others, and for which you have the means, says the wise writer of Proverbs. Don't put off until tomorrow the things that you can do today – do them now, so that your deeds will underscore your faith.

Father, open my eyes to the people around me who need my help right now and give me the courage to help them without delay. Amen.

February 17

DO GOOD
FOR HIS SAKE

*"The King will reply, 'I tell you the truth,
whatever you did for one of the least of
these brothers of mine, you did for me.'"*

MATTHEW 25:40

*W*hen you read this verse do you find yourself digging
in your purse for some loose coins to give to a beggar?
Do you wonder, "What if this man or woman is one of
the 'least' that the Bible talks of?"

Treat other people the way that you would like to be
treated. God regards everything that you do for others as
if you were doing it – or not – for Him personally!

*Father, help me to share the blessings I have with others in
need. Amen.*

BE SERVANTS

*"Whoever wants to become great among
you must be your servant, and whoever
wants to be first must be your slave."*

MATTHEW 20:26-27

*J*esus was willing to take on the duties of a slave when He washed the feet of His disciples. How willing are you to jump in and help when other people have needs? To give some money is really easy, but to become actively involved in the needs of others is much more difficult.

God doesn't want His children to sit on the porch and watch the world go by, but to be servants. Are you prepared to get your hands dirty and to roll up your sleeves to help others?

Lord Jesus, I don't want to sit idly by while others suffer around me. Show me how I can help them. Amen.

February 19

DON'T BE TOO BUSY

*"Martha, Martha," the Lord answered, "you are
worried and upset about many things, but only one
thing is needed. Mary has chosen what is better,
and it will not be taken away from her."*

LUKE 10:41-42

Busy Martha probably had no idea how Jesus could
think that Mary, by sitting at His feet and listening to
Him speak, had chosen the better part. We too can become so busy with other things that little time remains
for God.

Don't ever become so busy working for God that you
don't have time to spend communicating with Him. Set
aside time each day to spend alone with God.

*God, I want to spend as much time with You as I can. Please
help me to find time every day to spend quality time in Your
presence. Amen.*

GOD'S SOLUTIONS

"Do not be afraid. Stand firm and you will see the deliverance the LORD will bring you today. The LORD will fight for you; you need only to be still."

EXODUS 14:13-14

*T*he Israelites saw no way out of the battle for power in which they were engaged with Pharaoh. But Moses looked past the annihilating forces of Egypt and saw God. And he knew that with God doing battle on their side, they would definitely be victorious.

God always fights on your side too. Not only does He give you the victory, but He can give you solutions for every one of your problems.

Father God, because of You, I don't have to be afraid when troubles come my way because You fight for me. Amen.

HEAVEN'S DOOR

*He who has the Son has life; he who does
not have the Son of God does not have life.*

1 JOHN 5:12

am the Gate. Anyone who goes through me will be cared for – will freely go in and out, and find pasture. A thief is only there to steal and kill and destroy. I came so they can have real and eternal life, more and better life than they ever dreamed of," says Jesus (John 10:9-10 *The Message*).

Without Jesus it is impossible to have eternal life, because He is the only door into heaven. If you want to live forever, you must believe in Jesus. Without Him eternal life is always out of reach – only He can unlock the door to heaven for you.

Father, help me to live each day in such a way that I will not lose out on eternal life. Amen.

INVITE GOD IN

"Here I am! I stand at the door and knock.
If anyone hears my voice and opens the door,
I will come in and eat with him, and he with me."

REVELATION 3:20

*G*od really wants to come and make His home with you. That is why He knocks on the door of your heart. But the choice is yours. Only you can open the door. If you hear His voice and ask Him in, He will come in and live with you forever. That you can be certain of! And together with God life will be a constant celebration!

Don't put off opening the door of your heart and life to Him.

Jesus Christ, I open my heart to You. I give my life, my heart, my soul to You. Please come into my life and bless me with Your presence forever. Amen.

February 23

JESUS MAKES YOU NEW

Therefore, if anyone is in Christ, he is a new creation;
the old has gone, the new has come! All this is
from God, who reconciled us to himself through
Christ and gave us the ministry of reconciliation.

2 CORINTHIANS 5:17-18

Anyone who is in Christ is a brand new person – so writes Paul to the congregation in Corinth. "A new life burgeons" as *The Message* translation puts it. And this newness of life is God's work, not because of something you do.

When you surrender your life to God, Jesus makes you into a new person with new characteristics. That means that you should begin to act differently. Live in such a way that people can see that you are a brand new person!

Father God, make me into a new person. Help me to live in
such a way that everyone will be able to see that I am a new
person in You. Amen.

YOUR CHOICE

*"But if serving the L*ORD *seems undesirable to you, then choose for yourselves this day whom you will serve, whether the gods your forefathers served beyond the River, or the gods of the Amorites, in whose land you are living. But as for me and my household, we will serve the L*ORD*."*

JOSHUA 24:15

$\mathcal{J}$oshua gave the people a choice: they needed to decide once and for all if they would serve the one true God or the foreign gods. With great fanfare, the people chose God – but it wasn't long before they turned away from the God whom they had chosen.

The same is true of many of us. Today God gives you the chance to choose once again. The choice to allow Him into your life is your own. No one else can make the decision for you. Who do you choose?

Lord, I choose You. Please help me to turn back to You, to serve You and to live according to Your will always. $\mathcal{A}$men.

GLAD TIDINGS

"But you will receive power when the Holy Spirit comes on you; and you will be my witnesses in Jerusalem, and in all Judea and Samaria, and to the ends of the earth."

ACTS 1:8

*J*esus promised His twelve disciples that the Holy Spirit would equip them to tell other people about Him – in the communities in which they lived, in the countries in which they lived and even to the ends of the earth.

God also calls you to be His witness. How can you keep the good news of Jesus to yourself? The Holy Spirit will give you the courage and words you need to share it with others. In doing so, you'll also help carry the Good News to the ends of the earth.

God, through Your Spirit, give me the strength, courage and confidence to share the good news of Jesus with those around me. Amen.

THE LONGER YOU ARE A CHRISTIAN …

But grow in the grace and knowledge of our Lord and Savior Jesus Christ. To him be glory both now and forever! Amen.

2 PETER 3:18

We can never stop learning more about Jesus. Through studying His Word and the way He lived His life we will learn more and more about Him. And so we discover more and more about His grace.

The longer you are a Christian, the better you will learn to know Jesus, the more you will love Him and the more His characteristics will become visible in your life. Make sure that you grow spiritually each day.

Lord God, I want to get to know You more and more. Draw me closer to You so that I can follow in Your footsteps every day. Amen.

SPIRITUALLY MATURE

... Until we all reach unity in the faith and in the knowledge of the Son of God and become mature, attaining to the whole measure of the fullness of Christ.

EPHESIANS 4:13

*B*eing spiritually mature means that you will become more and more dependent on God. Then each day you will decrease, set aside the sins of the old man and become more like Jesus in your actions. Then you will be like a fully mature person, as perfect and complete as Jesus Himself.

Eventually you will be able to say, together with Paul, "I no longer live, but Christ lives in me" (Gal. 2:20).

Father, help me to die to my sinful nature so that I can grow spiritually and bear fruit for You. Amen.

FRUIT OF YOUR LABOR

*For we are God's fellow workers; you are
God's field, God's building. ... Always give
yourselves fully to the work of the Lord,
because you know that your labor
in the Lord is not in vain.*

1 CORINTHIANS 3:9, 15:58

*E*ach child of God is called to work for Him full time.
Therefore each of us should know the hope to which we
have been called and hold fast to what we believe. We
should never lose our enthusiasm. If there is something
that you can do for God, you should do it.

Although you often do not immediately see the fruit
of your labor, what you do for the Lord is always worth
the effort. Don't be tempted to become slack in your
commitment to His work.

*Father, I get discouraged when I do my best and nothing
seems to go right. But I know that You see my hard work and
You will let everything work out for the best.* *Amen.*

February 29

DO IT FOR THE
GLORY OF GOD

*So whether you eat or drink or whatever
you do, do it all for the glory of God.*

1 CORINTHIANS 10:31

*I*f you learn to do all that you do as if you were doing
it for God Himself, it will eventually make a tremendous
difference in your life.

Other people will see that God comes first in your life.
Your daily chores will even become much more pleasant
for you when you do them to the glory of God.

Ask the Lord to bless your work. And make absolutely
certain that you do nothing that will harm or damage
other people.

*Lord, I want to do everything to Your glory. I dedicate my
work, my life to You. Amen.*

March

BE STRONG AND COURAGEOUS!

Say to those with fearful hearts, "Be strong, do not fear;
your God will come, he will come with vengeance;
with divine retribution he will come to save you."

ISAIAH 35:4

It is not unusual these days to meet many people who want to throw in the towel because of all the negative things that happen around them. The prophet Isaiah has a message of comfort for such people: God says that they must be strong, and that they need fear nothing because He is with them.

If you are sitting in the depths of despair today, you can be strong and courageous. God knows about each one of your problems, and puts His strength at your disposal. And because He is with you, daily crises need never get the better of you.

No matter what happens around me, Lord, I will never lose hope, because You are always with me. You give me the courage and strength I need to go on. Amen.

SLEEP IN PEACE

I will not fear the tens of thousands
drawn up against me on every side.

PSALM 3:6

*T*he writer of Psalm 3 has a very positive testimony. He does not have to lie awake all night, tossing and turning while mulling over his problems. He sleeps peacefully each night and wakes up worry free because of the assurance that the Lord cares for Him and strengthens him. Therefore he can handle any crises in his life.

Does worry sometimes keep you awake at night? From now on you can sleep in peace: your God can and will provide for your every need!

Father, I lay all my worries at Your feet, knowing that You will provide everything I need. Amen.

PEACEFUL OASIS

My soul finds rest in God alone; my salvation
comes from him. He alone is my rock and my salvation;
he is my fortress, I will never be shaken.

PSALM 62:1-2

The world today is beset by a spirit of restlessness. But Christians have a peace that comes from deep within because they can trust in God at all times. He delivers us in times of need, and is our source of strength when things get too much for us to handle.

God wants to be your oasis of peace in a chaotic world. You can always find help and refuge in Him. All that you need to do is to trust Him.

Lord, You are my Source of peace. I trust You and turn to You for refuge when crises come my way. Amen.

GOD PROTECTS

You hem me in – behind and before;
you have laid your hand upon me.

PSALM 139:5

*G*od surrounds His children: He goes before them to show them the way, beside them to help them along their journey through life, behind them to protect them from dangers, and above them to pour out His blessings on them.

Even if you face dangers every day, God still hems you in on all sides. He will protect and keep you. Nothing that can do you lasting harm can penetrate the shield of His protection that surrounds His children.

Thank You, Father, for Your love and protection. *Amen.*

ANCHORED IN FAITH

Give thanks in all circumstances,
for this is God's will for you in Christ Jesus.

1 THESSALONIANS 5:18

God doesn't just ask His children to be thankful, but to be thankful in all things, including those things that they would have liked to have been different: the things that cause them pain and the things that they cannot understand.

The secret of the Christian's thankfulness is that it does not depend on his circumstances, but is anchored in his faith. Trust in God's will for your life and believe that He has only the best in store for you.

Even when things don't go my way, Lord, I know that I can still rejoice because I have You by my side and You will help me. Amen.

GOD'S LOVE FOR YOU

He replied, "You give them something to eat."
They answered, "We have only five loaves
of bread and two fish – unless we go and
buy food for all this crowd."

LUKE 9:13-14

When Jesus' disciples asked Him where they were to get enough food to feed the thousands of hungry people who had been listening to Him, they received a surprising answer: He told them that they should find food because it was their responsibility to care for the crowds.

God expects you to minister to the needs of the less privileged around you. What you do for Christ is the mirror in which others can see the love of God in your life – and your love for Him.

Jesus, open my eyes to where I can serve You today. Amen.

YOUR LOVE FOR GOD

"And if anyone gives even a cup of cold water to one of these little ones because he is my disciple, I tell you the truth, he will certainly not lose his reward."

MATTHEW 10:42

*I*f you truly love God, then you will also love other people and their needs will touch your heart, compelling you to do something to help them. When we help those who have less than we do, we indirectly help God and He will reward us.

The extent of your love for God is measured in the way in which you treat other people – especially those who are unable to return any favors.

Father God, help me to follow Jesus' example in loving and caring for those around me. Amen.

A FREE GIFT

"But love your enemies, do good to them, and lend to them without expecting to get anything back. Then your reward will be great, and you will be sons of the Most High, because he is kind to the ungrateful and wicked."

LUKE 6:35

*J*esus asks those who follow Him to love their enemies and do good to them, without expecting anything in return. It is very hard to get this right, but those who do manage it will receive a great reward: they will be called children of God.

If you do something for someone else, it should be freely given, not something that will somehow be of advantage to you. Then God Himself will reward you for it.

Lord Jesus, don't let my right hand see what my left hand is doing when I give to someone else. Let me never give with an expecting heart, rather let me give with love and thanksgiving to You. Amen.

YOUR OWN SINS

*"Why do you look at the speck of sawdust
in your brother's eye and pay no attention
to the plank in your own eye?"*

LUKE 6:41

People are inclined to look at their own sins through dark glasses, and the sins of others through the lens of a microscope. When you do something wrong it is never really bad in your own eyes, but if someone else were to do the exact same thing, you would probably find it unforgivable.

Make an effort from now on to treat other people as you would like them to treat you, and judge them in the same way that you would like to be judged.

God, help me to treat others the way I want to be treated, not judging anyone but loving them and forgiving them their sins like You forgive me mine. Amen.

SWEEP YOUR OWN FRONT PORCH

"How can you say to your brother, 'Brother, let me take the speck out of your eye,' when you yourself fail to see the plank in your own eye? You hypocrite, first take the plank out of your eye, and then you will see clearly to remove the speck from your brother's eye."

LUKE 6:42

People who have double standards are nothing more than hypocrites. Look carefully at your own faults, and do what you can to put them right. Only then will you have the right to address the faults of others. At the same time you will learn to be more understanding of their weaknesses. Not one of us is without fault!

In other words, sweep your own front porch before you check to see if your neighbor's yard is clean.

Father, give me the wisdom and the understanding to realize that I too have sinned. Help me to first repent of my own sins before I try to help others see theirs. Amen.

PUT YOUR HAND IN THE HAND OF JESUS

But when he saw the wind, he was afraid and,
beginning to sink, cried out, "Lord, save me!"
Immediately Jesus reached out his hand and caught him.
"You of little faith," he said, "why did you doubt?"

MATTHEW 14:30-31

When Peter saw that he was going to sink under the waves, he called to Jesus to help him. And Jesus was immediately ready to reach out a helping hand. But, He still admonished Peter for his lack of faith.

If it seems as though you are drowning in the sea of your circumstances, put your hand in Jesus' hand – He will deliver you from trouble every time. But make sure that you have faith and believe that He will do so.

Lord, in the midst of my troubles You reach out Your hand and guide me through. Amen.

SPIRITUALLY FIT

*Consider it pure joy, my brothers, whenever you
face trials of many kinds, because you know that
the testing of your faith develops perseverance.
Perseverance must finish its work so that you may
be mature and complete, not lacking anything.*

JAMES 1:2-4

*N*ot one of us likes our faith to be tested through
times of suffering, but hard times provide good exercise
for Christians. They increase our faith. Negative things in
our lives test how much we really trust God, and teach us
to live closer to Him.

Hard times are never pleasant, but they exercise your
faith, making you spiritually fit – through trials your faith
gets stronger and you learn to persevere.

*Lord, when times are tough, help me to persevere and to re-
main steadfast in my faith. Amen.*

HE WILL CARRY YOU

*There you saw how the LORD your God
carried you, as a father carries his son, all
the way you went until you reached this place.*

DEUTERONOMY 1:31

God was physically present with His people during all their years of wandering in the wilderness: as a cloud by day and a pillar of fire by night. He provided for every one of their needs.

God is still with His children each day, and He will carry us when we feel we cannot go any further. God goes ahead of you on your path through life. He will provide for every one of your needs and carry you through areas in your life when problems get you down and you feel you cannot go on.

When I can no longer walk, Lord, You are there to carry me. You are there to take care of me and to give me everything I need. Thank You, Lord. Amen.

YOUR RELATIONSHIP WITH THE LORD

"If you keep your feet from breaking the Sabbath and from doing as you please on my holy day, if you call the Sabbath a delight and the LORD's holy day honorable, ... then you will find your joy in the LORD, and I will cause you to ride on the heights of the land and to feast on the inheritance of your father Jacob."

ISAIAH 58:13-14

There are very few Christians today who treat Sundays the way God prescribes in His Word. What do you do on Sundays?

What you do on Sundays should be an indication of your relationship with the Lord. It is the one day in the week that you should set aside for Him and not focus on other things. If you do this, you will find a true and wonderful joy in His presence.

Father, help me to keep Your day holy, to rest in Your presence and to praise Your name. Amen.

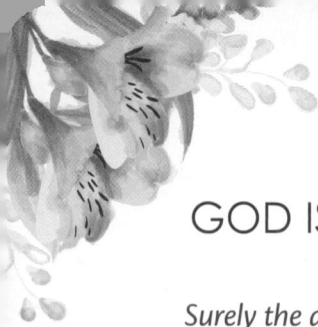

GOD IS ABLE TO HELP

*Surely the arm of the LORD is not too
short to save, nor his ear too dull to hear.*

ISAIAH 59:1

During the Exile, the people of God were constantly reminded of His promises, which He constantly renewed. He promised to help and rescue them in spite of the fact that they had so often turned away from Him.

God is just the same today as He was during biblical times. He still wants to help His children and listen to their problems. Even if your problems are beyond human help and your difficulties insurmountable, God is able to help. Nothing is impossible for Him.

Father, even if I face an impossible task, I know that I will be okay because anything is possible with You. Amen.

JESUS
CONQUERED DEATH

When the perishable has been clothed with the imperishable, and the mortal with immortality, then the saying that is written will come true: "Death has been swallowed up in victory." ... But thanks be to God! He gives us the victory through our Lord Jesus Christ.

1 CORINTHIANS 15:54, 57

*M*ost people are fearful of dying – possibly because death is such an unknown entity. When Jesus rose from the dead, He was able to put an end to the fear of death. He took the sting out of death's tail, said Paul.

Therefore, you need no longer be afraid of death. Jesus has already conquered it. Death for you is simply stepping into the Father's House where you will live happily together with Jesus forever.

Jesus, thank You for conquering death on my behalf and securing a place for me in heaven. Amen.

GIVE A SMILE!

All the days of the oppressed are wretched,
but the cheerful heart has a continual feast.

PROVERBS 15:15

Some people go through life with long faces. They find nothing beautiful or pleasant around them. And things seem to go wrong for them all the time. Thankfully, there are also the joyful people who find something in each day that they can be glad about. And life is a continual feast for such people, as the wise writer of Proverbs pointed out.

Make sure that you are a cheerful person. Keep a lookout for the things in each day that can bring you joy – and if you should see someone without a smile, give them one of yours!

Father, help me to find joy in each new day, focusing on Your presence and blessing in my life. Amen.

GOD IS WONDERFUL

"Be still, and know that I am God."

PSALM 46:10

*N*o one seems to have enough time these days – no time for themselves, no time for each other, and no time for God. Our lives are a mad rush from one appointment to another, from one commitment to another – and all the while we become spiritually poorer.

The time has come to slow down. Set aside at least half an hour a day to be quiet before God. Meditate on His wonder and might and praise Him for His grace and mercy toward you.

The more time I spend in Your presence, Lord, the more I realize that the most valuable part of any day is that precious time with You. Amen.

YOU ARE PRECIOUS

"Since you are precious and honored in my sight, and because I love you, I will give men in exchange for you, and people in exchange for your life."

ISAIAH 43:4

It is easy to develop an inferiority complex if you keep comparing yourself to friends who are prettier, thinner, and more talented than you are. In the process you quickly forget how highly God regards you. He Himself says that He loves you, that He thinks highly of you, that He has made you in His image and He knows your name.

When you feel as if no one respects you, remember that God sees you as eternally precious.

Father, help me to look at myself through Your eyes, realizing that my worth lies in You and not in what other people think or say. Amen.

FRIENDSHIP IS PRECIOUS

A man of many companions may come to ruin,
but there is a friend who sticks closer than a brother.

PROVERBS 18:24

$\mathcal{I}$t sometimes happens that people whom we trust betray our trust. If you have ever been hurt in this way, it becomes more difficult to trust other people the next time. But then you discover that there are friends who will never let you down. They never disappoint you, and are always there when you need them.

Friendship is precious. Treasure the friends that you have, and nurture them. And always remember: before you can have a friend, you need to be a friend.

Thank You, God, for the friends You've given me. Help me to be the friend to others that I wish they would be for me.

Amen.

JESUS WILL NEVER LEAVE YOU

"Greater love has no one than this, that he lay down his life for his friends. You are my friends if you do what I command."

JOHN 15:13-14

*T*here is no one who is perfect. Therefore you can count on it that even your best friend will let you down at times. Jesus, however, is the one Friend who will always be with you, who will never disappoint you and who will never leave you, who loves you so much that He even gave His life so that you can live.

And today He comes to you to tell you that you can be His friend, if you are prepared do the things that He asks in His Word.

Lord Jesus, You are the best Friend anyone could ask for. You are always there for me, always love me and even gave Your life to save me. Thank You, Lord. Amen.

GOD WILL CARRY YOU

*"You yourselves have seen what I did to Egypt,
and how I carried you on eagles' wings
and brought you to myself."*

EXODUS 19:4

*G*od led His people safely through the wilderness. He uses the image of an eagle and its young to describe His protective love of His people. Just as an eagle flies beneath its young to prevent them from falling while they are learning to fly, God will carry His people safely on eagle's wings.

This promise is directed at you too: God will protect you today, and He wants to carry you through the hard times just as an eagle carries its young.

Father God, thank You for taking care of us like an eagle takes care of her eaglets. Amen.

YOUR ENTHUSIASM MIGHT WANE

*Never be lacking in zeal, but keep
your spiritual fervor, serving the Lord.*

ROMANS 12:11

*W*hen you are newly born again, you are usually enthusiastic for the things of the Lord. Nothing is too much trouble for you. You set aside much time for your personal devotions, you go to church often, and you pray without ceasing. Sometimes this early dedication diminishes, but it should not.

It is a typical human reaction for the initial enthusiasm for the things of the Lord to lessen. Make sure that this does not happen to you.

Father, help me to have faith like a child, enthusiastically serving You and spending time praying and studying Your Word. Amen.

YOUR LIFE
SHOULD CHANGE

All Scripture is God-breathed and is useful for teaching, rebuking, correcting and training in righteousness.

2 TIMOTHY 3:16

The Bible has a deep influence on your whole life. It helps you to help others who have wandered from God's path; it helps you to discern between what is right and wrong; it also teaches you how God expects you to live and what He expects from you.

It is not enough simply to have a good knowledge of biblical facts. The Word of God should change your life for the better. Live as the Bible asks you to!

Lord, I don't merely want to know what the Bible says, I want it to change the way I live. Help me to soak in Your Word and to make it a part of every area of my life. Amen.

THE HOLY SPIRIT AS TEACHER

I keep asking that the God of our Lord Jesus Christ, the glorious Father, may give you the Spirit of wisdom and revelation, so that you may know him better.

EPHESIANS 1:17

When you open the Bible, God will speak personally to you, and He sends His Holy Spirit to explain the Scriptures to you. The Spirit of God gives you the necessary wisdom so that you can understand the Word.

Without the Holy Spirit teaching you, you will not be able to fully grasp the message of the Bible. He is the only Person who can give you real insight into God's Word. Ask Him now to help you when you read the Bible.

Father God, give me an understanding of Your Word so that I can live out Your will for my life. Amen.

GOD'S WORD

*Let the word of Christ dwell in you richly as you
teach and admonish one another with all wisdom,
and as you sing psalms, hymns and spiritual
songs with gratitude in your hearts to God.*

COLOSSIANS 3:16

Every word in the Bible comes from God Himself.
Therefore, you should never be satisfied until you know
everything that He wants you to know. Study the Bible
so that you can really know what it says. Make time to
study the Bible in depth, using concordances and different Bible translations.

If you also make the effort to learn key passages by
heart, you will always have God's Word with you, and it
will become a precious, inextricable part of your life.

*Father, help me to study Your Word, to understand it and to
keep Your decrees in my heart.* Amen.

GOD'S LAW

*Teach them the decrees and laws, and show them the
way to live and the duties they are to perform.*

EXODUS 20: 18:20

$\mathcal{S}$ome people do not like the Ten Commandments.
They think they are a set of stifling rules and regulations
that God has instituted to keep them in check. Nothing
could be further from the truth. God's law is the road
map that He provides for His children. It tells you what
road to follow if you want to live a life of true joy.

Look at God's commandments again and allow them
to point out the road for you to travel.

*Lord, I pray that Your commandments will be the compass
to point out the road ahead. Amen.*

NOTHING IS AS IMPORTANT AS GOD

"I am the LORD your God, who brought you
out of Egypt, out of the land of slavery.
You shall have no other gods before me."

EXODUS 20:2-3

God does not tolerate His people turning from Him to worship idols. He wants you to serve Him only. He wants to be your only God. Even though He regularly renewed His covenant of love with His people, they still often turned from Him to worship foreign gods.

Even though we no longer worship statues of gods, anything that is more important in our lives than God Himself is an idol. Make sure that there is nothing in your life that means more than your relationship with God.

Lord, help me to get rid of everything in my life that could possibly become an idol. I want to be completely focused on and dedicated to You. Amen.

March 29

GOD IS ALMIGHTY

The earth is the LORD's, and everything in it,
the world, and all who live in it.

PSALM 24:1

*G*od is the Creator of all things. He created the world and all that is in it, He maintains it day by day, and therefore the earth and everything in it belongs to God.

The God you worship is almighty and can do all things. Even though you live in a world of unrest and violence, your future, and that of your children, is safe in His hands. He is mighty to save you from any danger and promises to always protect you.

Creator God, I stand in awe of Your creation. Thank You for the beautiful world You have blessed us with. Amen.

LOVE AND FEAR

*There is no fear in love. But perfect love drives out
fear, because fear has to do with punishment.
The one who fears is not made perfect in love.*

1 JOHN 4:18

It is impossible to love God and to trust Him, and yet still be afraid and worried about many things. If you love God above all things, there will not be space in your life for fear to get a foothold.

Make a list of all the things of which you are afraid, the things that cause you stress and the things that you are worried about and then give the list to God. Love and fear cannot exist side by side, so trust Him to give you peace and strength to face any difficulty.

*In Your love, Lord, You take away all my fears, my worries
and my cares. I refuse to go one more day worrying about
what I cannot control. You are in control and I trust in You.*

Amen.

WITH JESUS
AT YOUR SIDE

I can do everything through him who gives me strength.

PHILIPPIANS 4:13

*P*aul was an exceptional man who attempted unbelievable things. The reason he could do what he did is because God gave him the strength to succeed (Phil. 4:13).

Jesus wants to be a source of strength for you today and His strength is at your disposal. Be strong and courageous: if He is with you, there is absolutely nothing that you and He together cannot do.

Lord Jesus, with You by my side I can do anything. Amen.

April

GOD HAS NO FAVORITES

*And masters, treat your slaves in the same way.
Do not threaten them, since you know that he
who is both their Master and yours is in heaven,
and there is no favoritism with him.*

EPHESIANS 6:9

Sometimes, unintentionally, we feel that God favors other people over us – people we think are better than us. But that cannot be, affirms Paul to the church at Ephesus. We all worship the same God, and God has no favorites. He treats each one of His children in exactly the same way.

Take Paul's words to heart and make sure that you don't favor some people above others. Try to treat everyone you come into contact with in exactly the same way.

God, I know that You are absolutely fair and just. You treat all of us in exactly the same way. Help me to do the same.

Amen.

GOD IS OUR ROCK

The LORD is a refuge for the oppressed,
a stronghold in times of trouble.

PSALM 9:9

When we turn on the TV or open a newspaper, it seems that danger is all around us. People are robbed, assaulted and murdered. We don't feel safe anywhere. And so we live behind fences and walls and are sometimes even afraid to open our front doors.

But God is still a Rock for His children to which they can flee in times of trouble, just as He was when the psalmist wrote these words – He can protect you from any danger.

Father, I run to You for refuge when troubles come my way. I trust in Your protection and strength. Amen.

WAIT FOR HIS ANSWER

*My heart is not proud, O Lord, my eyes are not
haughty; I do not concern myself with great matters
or things too wonderful for me. But I have stilled and
quieted my soul; like a weaned child with its mother,
like a weaned child is my soul within me.*

PSALM 131:1-2

There are many things that happen to us that we cannot understand. We have dozens of "why?" questions that don't receive any answers. But it isn't always necessary for us to understand the way God acts.

God's children do not need to tire themselves out over things that they do not understand. They can rest safely in God's arms and wait for His answers. Do this next time you need answers – spend some quiet time with Him and trust He will supply you with what you need.

Lord God, I trust You to lead me on the path that is the best way to travel through this world for me. Amen.

GOD ALWAYS ANSWERS

When I called, you answered me;
you made me bold and stouthearted.

PSALM 138:3

When we pray, God will answer – but sometimes He answers in His own time and in His own way, and that means that sometimes His answer is not what we would have chosen it to be.

If you have been praying for a long time about an issue and do not yet have an answer, keep on praying. God is there, and He hears you. He will answer your prayer and give you the strength you need as you wait for the answer. Rest in His answer – it is the right one for you.

Father, I know that no matter when or where I pray, You will answer. Amen.

SERENITY

Therefore my heart is glad and my tongue rejoices; my body also will rest secure. ... You have made known to me the path of life; you will fill me with joy in your presence, with eternal pleasures at your right hand.

PSALM 16:9, 11

*A*s Christians, we can live with serenity and a song in our hearts. We are always safe because we trust in God; we rejoice in the grace and in the guidance that He gives us in our lives. It is when we are close to Him that we are filled with joy.

You too can live with peace in your heart when you leave your problems in God's hands.

Because of You, Lord, I can wake up every morning with a song in my heart. You give me grace and guide my steps. Because You are with me, I can rejoice. Amen.

GOD IS ALWAYS
THE SAME

*Jesus Christ is the same yesterday
and today and forever.*

HEBREWS 13:8

Each day we see how things around us change. Technology, science, politics, the economy and world opinions. The truth is that we can be absolutely certain of nothing. Except God. He is the same yesterday, today and for all time. He is the only One who cannot change.

Therefore, you don't need to learn to trust God anew each day. He is always the same. He has proved His faithfulness in the past.

Thank You, Lord for never changing. Thank You for remaining the faithful, loving and forgiving Father we've always known.

Amen.

HARD TIMES

This poor man called, and the LORD heard him;
he saved him out of all his troubles.

PSALM 34:6

Many times God uses your difficulties as a platform from which you can bear testimony of His goodness. It is more difficult to trust God and rejoice in Him during hard times than when things are going well. But God makes it possible for us to be filled with His joy even in the midst of troubles.

You can rejoice because God holds you in the palm of His hand and you know for sure that He will help you now, just as He has always done in the past.

Heavenly Father, even in times of tribulation I can rejoice, knowing that You are with me and will help me. Amen.

April 8

TRUE JOY

Blessed is the man who does not walk in the counsel of the wicked or stand in the way of sinners or sit in the seat of mockers. But his delight is in the law of the LORD, and on his law he meditates day and night.

PSALM 1:1-2

When you open your Bible you meet God Himself and He gives you His joy. God's children find joy when they are assured of His love and mercy in His Word, and time after time hear His voice speaking personally to them as they read it.

The secret of true joy is to find your joy in the Word of God, rather than in the pleasures of this world. Make time each day to read the Bible and reflect on God's words.

Lord, I seek my joy in Your Word, in Your presence, rather than the pleasures of the world that are here one day and gone the next. Amen.

POSSESSIONS

*Better what the eye sees than
the roving of the appetite.*

ECCLESIASTES 6:9

Many people work hard day and night to accumulate money and material possessions. But money and possessions cannot guarantee your happiness. To be happy is to be satisfied with the things that you have. True joy comes from knowing for certain that you have a heavenly Father who can see to your every need.

If your happiness is dependent on your possessions, you will never have enough. Value and enjoy the things that you do have, rather than desiring more.

Lord God, thank You for all the wonderful blessings You've given me. Amen.

WORK IS A PRIVILEGE

*Then I realized that it is good and proper for a
man to eat and drink, and to find satisfaction in
his toilsome labor under the sun during the few
days of life God has given him – for this is his lot.*

ECCLESIASTES 5:18

Sometimes we complain that the amount of work we
have to do keeps us busy for hours. But work is satisfy-
ing and enriching. To be able to work is a privilege. The
ability to be able to work, as well as the enthusiasm to do
your work joyfully, are gifts from God.

If you have a job that allows you to use your talents,
do it as if you were doing it for God and remember to
work with joy in your heart. Your work is a gift from God.

*Heavenly Father, help me to use my talents every day to Your
service and to Your glory. Amen.*

USE TODAY

Do not say, "Why were the old days better than these?"
For it is not wise to ask such questions.

ECCLESIASTES 7:10

$\mathcal{S}$ome people long nostalgically for the past when everything, according to them, was so much better than now. They are never satisfied with anything in the present – not the social conditions, the cost of living or the political situation.

If you are one of those people who long for "the good old days", you need to make a paradigm shift. Guard against always living in the past. That is foolishness, says Ecclesiastes. Set your hope on the future and use today to really live life to the full.

Father, help me to live each day to the full, taking a hold of every opportunity and making the best use of my time.

Amen.

April 12

USE EVERY OPPORTUNITY

Whatever your hand finds to do,
do it with all your might.

ECCLESIASTES 9:10

Each day dozens of opportunities come your way. Sometimes you are too tired and sometimes just too lazy to grab hold of them, and so you let them slip past you – only to be sorry later that you did so. Learn to live in such a way that you get the most out of life.

Make the most of every opportunity that comes your way, work hard, and enjoy it – you might never again get the chance that you waste today.

Heavenly Father, help me to live each day to the full, not wasting a single opportunity You give me. Amen.

April 13

FAITH BRINGS RESULTS

"That is why I did not even consider myself worthy to come to you. But say the word, and my servant will be healed." ... When Jesus heard this, he was amazed at him, and turning to the crowd following him, he said, "I tell you, I have not found such great faith even in Israel."

LUKE 7:7, 9

When people came to Jesus with requests and supplications, He first looked to see if they really believed that He could do the things that they asked of Him. If He saw that they did believe in Him, then He gladly granted their requests.

Do you believe that God can answer your prayers? Faith always brings results. And a strong faith is never your own doing – it is a response to the greatness of God.

Jesus Christ, I believe. Help my unbelief. Amen.

FAITH SAVES

For in Christ Jesus neither circumcision nor uncircumcision has any value. The only thing that counts is faith expressing itself through love.

GALATIANS 5:6

When you become a Christian, your life changes. You are now a new person. What should be important to you now is that your faith will be made evident by the things that you do in love for others.

You are saved by faith, but once you are saved, you demonstrate your faith in the things that you do – then the great deeds that God asks of you will follow – as an offering of thanks for the fact that God has saved you.

Lord, let my actions show my love for You and faith in You as my Lord and Savior. Amen.

OFFER OF GRACE

For their sake he remembered his covenant
and out of his great love he relented.

PSALM 106:45

We read in many places in the Old Testament how God demonstrated His covenant to His disobedient nation. Since He loved them, He was always ready to help them.

On the cross God demonstrated His love for you and offered you his grace. You need to respond personally to this offer of grace. Have you done so? If you have, He will also be prepared to forgive your sins and to show by His grace how much He loves you.

Father, I humbly accept Your offer of grace. Thank You for sacrificing everything just to save me. Amen.

TRUE FAITH

He withdrew about a stone's throw beyond them, knelt down and prayed, "Father, if you are willing, take this cup from me; yet not my will, but yours be done."

LUKE 22:41-42

In Gethsemane, Jesus prayed so earnestly for God to remove the cup of suffering from Him that His sweat fell like drops of blood to the ground. Because He was completely human, He could not see His way clear to endure the inhuman suffering that was awaiting Him. Yet He was willing to rest in His Father's will.

True faith means seeking God's will in prayer, not forcing your opinion on Him.

Lord God, I want to surrender my will to You completely, like Jesus did in Gethsemane. Amen.

HOPE

*But if we hope for what we do not
yet have, we wait for it patiently.*

ROMANS 8:25

We like to say that seeing is believing. But God wants His children to hope in those things that they cannot yet see. He wants them to be so certain of His promises that they will hold fast to them, even though they have not yet seen them come to fulfillment.

Hope is the steadfast trust that the things that you desire will one day be a reality. And you will never be ashamed when you hope in God. Persevere in hope!

*Heavenly Father, give us the perseverance to cling to the hope
we have and the patience to wait for Your perfect timing.*

Amen.

GOD'S PROMISES

*The LORD is good to those whose hope
is in him, to the one who seeks him.*

LAMENTATIONS 3:25

For the person who lives in hope, the future is full of promise – the promise that God's promises will definitely come to pass.

And Christians have the assurance that there is a future for them in heaven with God. That all the difficulties of the present will be done away with forever, and that only the joy of God will remain.

The new heaven and the new earth that God has promised will be a reality for them.

Father, I hold on to the hope of the new heaven and new earth You've promised. Amen.

GLORY IN HEAVEN

Be joyful in hope, patient in affliction, faithful in prayer.

ROMANS 12:12

Paul encouraged the Christians in Rome to look forward with joy to the day when God will make all things new. He told them not to lose hope in hard times, and not to stop praying.

Make it your resolution this year to live in hope and to cling to God in times of crisis. Christians can endure hard times far better than unbelievers because they live with hope in their hearts – the hope of glory that awaits them in heaven.

I live in hope, Lord, because I believe in Your promise of the glory that awaits me in heaven. Until then, I cling to You in all my troubles. Amen.

GOD KNOWS ABOUT YOUR PROBLEMS

Why do you say, O Jacob, and complain, O Israel, "My way is hidden from the Lord; my cause is disregarded by my God"? … The Lord is the everlasting God, the Creator of the ends of the earth. He will not grow tired or weary, and his understanding no one can fathom. But those who hope in the Lord will renew their strength.

ISAIAH 40:27-28, 31

Sometimes when we go through difficult times it seems as if God has forgotten about us. Thankfully, that is impossible. God is almighty. There is nothing that He does not know about.

Therefore, hold on to hope. God knows about each one of your problems. He sees your pain and offers you His love and help.

Thank You for being the almighty Father who sees everything. You know exactly what I am going through and You will help me. Amen.

FIND YOUR JOY
IN THE LORD

*Delight yourself in the Lord and he will give you
the desires of your heart. Commit your way
to the Lord; trust in him and he will do this.*

PSALM 37:4-5

People who live far from God try in vain to find joy in life. There are just too many negative things that make them despondent and tense. But for those who trust in God, joy is a way of life. They discover from day to day that God fulfills all their desires and gives them things they don't really need but that make life more pleasant.

Find your joy in the Lord. Yield your life to Him, trust in Him and He will give you the desires of your heart.

Lord Jesus, You are the source of joy and life. I pray that You will fill my life with Your love and joy. Amen.

April 22

TRUE JOY

*The ransomed of the L*ORD *will return. They will
enter Zion with singing; everlasting joy will crown
their heads. Gladness and joy will overtake them,
and sorrow and sighing will flee away.*

ISAIAH 35:10

Isaiah prophesied that the people who were taken away, weeping, into exile would return to Zion as people filled with joy. And it is the Lord who makes their return from exile, as well as their joy, possible.

God still wants to make His children happy. The secret of people who are always smiling is that they have Jesus in their lives. The joy that He gives cannot be hidden away: it radiates happiness all around.

*Heavenly Father, I rejoice in Your name! My heart is bursting
with joy in You.* Amen.

GOD'S PROMISES

*Not one of all the LORD's good promises to the
house of Israel failed; every one was fulfilled.*

JOSHUA 21:45

Joshua assured the people that God always does what
He has promised. Not even one of His promises can remain unfulfilled. Every promise will come to fruition.

God cannot ever be untrue to one of His promises.
You can believe with your whole heart that every promise God made in His Word that pertains to you will come
to pass if you believe in Him, just as it did for His people
long ago.

*Almighty Father, You are a faithful, caring and loving God.
Thank You for the assurance that Your promises for me will
come true. Amen.*

FAITH AND TRUST

"Therefore I tell you, whatever you ask for in prayer, believe that you have received it, and it will be yours."

MARK 11:24

*J*esus promised us that we would get those things that we ask for in prayer, if we believe that God will give them to us. If you pray and do not receive, accept that your request does not form part of God's plan for your life. But know too that He will always give you what is best for you.

Faith and trust go hand-in-hand: God's children should have faith in Him without harboring any doubt in their hearts that He will do what He has promised to do.

Father, remove any doubt that I might still have in my heart. I want to believe in You with all of my heart, all of my soul and all of my strength. Amen.

SUCCESS IS POSSIBLE

*Unless the LORD builds the house, its builders
labor in vain. Unless the LORD watches over the city,
the watchmen stand guard in vain. In vain you
rise early and stay up late, toiling for food to
eat – for he grants sleep to those he loves.*

PSALM 127:1-2

$\mathcal{T}$he psalmist knew a secret that we should make our own: together with God, success is within our reach. If He helps you, you cannot help but be a winner!

But the opposite is also true. All your hard work and effort is worth nothing if God is not involved in what you do. He is the one who makes success possible and easy for you. Acknowledge Him in all your ways and He will put His miracle-working power at your disposal.

Without You, Lord, I can do nothing. But in Your strength, I can conquer anything. Amen.

BE SENSITIVE TO THE FEELINGS OF OTHERS

My son, preserve sound judgment and discernment,
do not let them out of your sight; they will be life
for you, an ornament to grace your neck.

PROVERBS 3:21-22

People who know how to treat people without rubbing them up the wrong way, will go far in life. Learn to speak and act appropriately, to take others into account, and the chances are they will do the same to you.

Pay particular attention to your words. Think carefully before you speak. Be sensitive to others people's feelings, and don't say things that could cause permanent damage and that you will be sorry about later.

Lord, help me to treat others with kindness and compassion.
Let me only speak words of encouragement and love.

Amen.

BE PATIENT

Do nothing out of selfish ambition or vain conceit,
but in humility consider others better than yourselves.

PHILIPPIANS 2:3

It is innate to our human nature to always want to be first, and to see ourselves as more important than others. But that is not how God wants His children to behave. He expects us to be prepared to be the least important.

If other people's concerns carry more weight with you than your own, it will be easy to see when you do things wrong and so you will be willing to apologize and to be patient with others.

Father, help me to not let my pride get the better of me. I want to serve You and Your people in humility. Amen.

LOVE OTHERS

"A new command I give you: Love one another.
As I have loved you, so you must love one another."

JOHN 13:34

Our love for others should be a mirror image of Jesus' love for us. That is the essence of the new covenant that He gave to the world. And we will never be able to get it right without Him.

The love that God asks of you is not based on how good and nice the other person is, but it is to love them in spite of their faults and shortcomings. Ask God to give you this love through His Holy Spirit who lives in you.

Lord God, send Your Holy Spirit to fill my heart with Your love so that I can love others more than I love myself. Amen.

GOD'S
PATIENCE

The LORD appeared to us in the past, saying:
"I have loved you with an everlasting love;
I have drawn you with loving-kindness."

JEREMIAH 31:3

*G*od had all the patience in the world with His rebellious people. And His love for them knew no bounds. No matter how disloyal they were to Him, even though they turned away from Him time after time to worship foreign gods, His love for them remained constant and He was always prepared to give them another chance.

The Lord wants you to have just as much patience with others as He has with you. He wants you to be as loyal to them as He is to you.

Father, I am not a very patient person. Help me to show as much patience with others as You have shown with me.

Amen.

YOU BELONG TO GOD

Even though I walk through the valley of the
shadow of death, I will fear no evil, for you are
with me; your rod and your staff, they comfort me.

PSALM 23:4

*C*hildren of God can remain calm in the midst of danger because they trust in Him. They know without a doubt that He is with them and that He promises to carry them through dangerous times.

Because you belong to God, you can face each day with strength and courage. Because He is with you, you need fear nothing. God will carry you and deliver you, even through the valley of death. In His hands you are always safe.

Almighty God, because of You, I can face any challenge, any difficulty with strength and courage. Because You are with me, I need not fear. Amen.

May

HE FORGIVES

*In his distress he sought the favor of the
LORD his God and humbled himself
greatly before the God of his fathers.
And when he prayed to him, the LORD was moved
by his entreaty and listened to his plea; so he
brought him back to Jerusalem and to his kingdom.
Then Manasseh knew that the LORD is God.*

2 CHRONICLES 33:12-13

While King Manasseh was in exile, he confessed his sins before God and asked for His help. And God heard Manasseh's prayer. He allowed him to return to Jerusalem and to resume his reign of Judah.

God's mercy and forgiveness are indescribably great. He can and will forgive each one of your sins. If things go badly for you, confess your sins to God. He will forgive you and be gracious to you.

God of mercy, forgive me for I have sinned. Be gracious to me and wash away my sins. Amen.

HE WILL HELP YOU

What, then, shall we say in response to this? If God is for us, who can be against us? ... No, in all these things we are more than conquerors through him who loved us.

ROMANS 8:31, 37

God is on His children's side. Therefore, there is nothing that can really be to their disadvantage or get them down. Even in hopeless situations they can be victors, because God fights for them and He is unconquerable.

God wants to offer you His help. Even when bad things happen to you, if God is on your side, nothing can be against you. In Him you are always more than a conqueror. He will help and support you in every situation.

Lord, You are my refuge and strength. When troubles come my way, I run to You for safety and You help me. Amen.

May 3

FAITH MEANS TO
KEEP BELIEVING

*Now faith is being sure of what we hope
for and certain of what we do not see.*

HEBREWS 11:1

Faith means putting your doubts away for good. It means that you no longer insist on seeing visible signs of God's love and faithfulness, but that you will trust Him no matter how hard that may be, that you will keep hoping in Him even though you cannot see Him.

Faith is to keep believing, even when you cannot see; it is holding fast to God's promises even though you don't see one coming to pass. Faith makes the impossible possible.

Father, even though I cannot possibly see the future, I have faith that You will fulfill Your promises to me and let everything work out for the best. Amen.

GOD'S ALMIGHTY POWER

*Ignoring what they said, Jesus told the
synagogue ruler, "Don't be afraid; just believe."*

MARK 5:36

*J*esus asked Jairus to keep believing even when someone came to tell him that his daughter was dead. It seems
extremely unsympathetic to us, but Jesus had good reason to expect the impossible from Jairus – the Lord
would ensure that Jairus's faith would not be disappointed. He raised the little girl from the dead.

It is hard to keep hoping when all hope seems gone,
but if you can get it right, you will experience God's
almighty power in your life.

*Heavenly Father, when it seems all hope is lost, I can keep
on hoping, because nothing is impossible for You. Amen.*

GIVE THE GLORY TO GOD

Each one should use whatever gift he has received to serve others, faithfully administering God's grace in its various forms.

1 PETER 4:10

God made you in such a way that you can do certain things well and excel in certain areas, not to garner money and honor for yourself. He wants you to know that these things are gifts of His grace and you should give Him the honor and glory through them by serving others with those gifts.

You are a minister of God's grace. Live in such a way that other people can see Him in you, and will praise Him for the things you achieve.

Lord, help me to use my gifts in service of You and to Your glory. Amen.

A FLAME OF LOVE

We love because he first loved us.

1 JOHN 4:19

*L*ove is a quality that no person receives as an innate attribute. God makes it possible for us to love Him and He makes it possible for you to love other people. Love comes from Him and He loved us while we were yet sinners and living far from Him.

God's love should ignite a flame of love in your heart – a flame that will warm everyone around you.

Honor this gift from God by treating everyone with love and respect, irrespective of how they treat you.

Lord, ignite that flame of Your love in my heart. Allow it to warm the people around me so that, through me, they might see You. Amen.

COMPLETE TRUST

Cast all your anxiety on him because he cares for you.

1 PETER 5:7

People today are bowed down under the weight of countless anxieties. There are so many things that cause stress that about 90% of illnesses are attributed to excessive stress. And it is all so unnecessary. Become peaceful. Give your anxieties to God; He promises to care for you.

The definition of complete trust is bringing every one of your burdens to God, so that He can take over the care of them. Don't put it off any longer – do it right now!

Heavenly Father, I am filled with stress and worry about things I have no control over. I give You everything that makes me anxious. Take it from me and fill me with Your peace. Amen.

HE IS ALWAYS THERE

My help comes from the LORD, the Maker of heaven and earth. He will not let your foot slip – he who watches over you will not slumber.

PSALM 121:2-3

*G*od is a Helper for His children. He is always ready to help us, to come quickly to our aid and to protect us. In just about every psalm this fact is asserted.

Our Helper is almighty – not only is He the Creator of heaven and earth, He is also our personal God and always available for us. We can approach Him night and day with our problems and He will always be ready to help.

Thank You, Lord, for being there 24/7. Knowing that You are always with me fills me with such joy and peace. Amen.

OBEDIENCE TO GOD

*I rejoice in following your statutes
as one rejoices in great riches.*

PSALM 119:14

The writer of Psalm 119 uncovered a great truth: people who live according to the dictates of God's Word are happy people. To do what God asks you to do is the sure way to be happy every day. If you make God happy, you will be happy!

True joy is to obey God and to honor Him. His law points you in the right direction and it brings greater joy than worldly riches and recognition.

Father, I want to obey You in everything I do. Guide me on the right path and show me how to live in honor of You.

Amen.

IF YOU BELONG
TO GOD …

Rejoice in the Lord always. I will say it again: Rejoice!
Let your gentleness be evident to all. The Lord is near.

PHILIPPIANS 4:4-5

*B*eing happy is easy for the child of God. But even God's children struggle to be happy all the time. The closer we live to God, the easier it becomes to be filled with joy. We can be joyful because we are in His presence and we know that He cares for us.

If you belong to God, you can live with joy, even when things don't go well with you, because you know that God has His arms around you all the time.

Draw me closer to You, Lord. Allow me to experience the joy of being in Your presence. Amen.

JESUS PAID
ON THE CROSS

*In him we have redemption through his blood,
the forgiveness of sins, in accordance with the
riches of God's grace that he lavished on us
with all wisdom and understanding.*

EPHESIANS 1:7-8

When Jesus' blood flowed from the cross, it washed away the guilt of sin of those who believe in Him. God is willing to forgive our sins because Jesus reestablished peace between Him and us. We can never be grateful enough for this goodness of God.

Because Jesus paid the price of your sin on the cross, you can enjoy the riches of God's grace in your life each day, and live out of His abundance.

Jesus, thank You for offering up Your life so that I might live and be forgiven. Amen.

CLOSER TO GOD

*But how is it to your credit if you receive a
beating for doing wrong and endure it? But if
you suffer for doing good and you endure it,
this is commendable before God.*

1 PETER 2:20

When we deserve to be punished, it is easier to accept
our punishment. But when we are punished unfairly, if
we believe that we do not deserve to be punished, it is
much more difficult to accept it.

You might sometimes suffer because of things that
were not your fault. God will give you the grace to accept such suffering. Undeserved punishment can in itself
be an act of grace because it has the ability to bring you
closer to God.

*Father, whether I suffer for the things I have or have not done,
I will persevere, because You are with me. Amen.*

DEEDS OF LOVE

*"Bless those who curse you, pray for those
who mistreat you. ... Do to others as
you would have them do to you."*

LUKE 6:28, 31

God's love for you is indescribable – but because He loves you unconditionally, He expects you to love in the same way: that you will bless people who persecute you; that you will pray for those who seek to harm you. This sounds impossible to do, and so it is, but God makes it possible for you to love as He does.

God wants your love for Him to be translated into deeds of love – especially toward those people who least deserve it!

Father, please give me a heart for everyone, not just for those I like, but also those who want to do me harm. Amen.

GIVE GENEROUSLY

*Each man should give what he has decided
in his heart to give, not reluctantly or under
compulsion, for God loves a cheerful giver.*

2 CORINTHIANS 9:7

God does not have set regulations concerning the amounts we should give to Him – although a tenth was the expected amount in the Old Testament. He does not want us to feel under obligation to give some of our possessions and money to Him and others, but He wants us to give joyfully.

God loves people who are not stingy but who delight in giving to others. Ask Him to make you into a cheerful and generous giver.

Father God, please make me a cheerful giver, not just of money and possessions, but of my time as well. *Amen.*

GOD LIVES IN YOU

Splendor and majesty are before him;
strength and joy in his dwelling place.

1 CHRONICLES 16:27

*D*avid wrote a beautiful song of thanks for the Levites to sing before the ark of the Lord (see 1 Chr. 16:4-36). This song contrasts God's attributes with those of worthless people, and David comes to the conclusion that God is truly very great, that He is filled with glory and splendor, that strength and joy are found in His presence.

Joy is the legacy of God's children. Joy and peace fill the place that God inhabits continuously. And through His Spirit, God lives in you.

Father, I open my heart and my life anew to Your Spirit. Come live in my heart so that I too can experience Your wonderful joy and love. Amen.

GOD CARES FOR YOU

*"Until now you have not asked for anything
in my name. Ask and you will receive,
and your joy will be complete."*

JOHN 16:24

Shortly before Jesus was crucified, He explained to His disciples that believers have every reason to be glad. God ultimately changes the heartache of His children into gladness because He cares for us. If we come openly to God with our needs, He will hear our prayers and make our joy complete.

The awareness of God's love and care is an indisputable source of joy for all His children, including you.

Heavenly Father, I lay before You all my needs and wants. Let Your will be done in my life so that my joy can be complete.

Amen.

May 17

GOD GUARANTEES
A SAFE JOURNEY

*He stilled the storm to a whisper; the waves of
the sea were hushed. They were glad when it grew
calm, and he guided them to their desired haven.*

PSALM 107:29-30

In Psalm 107, the psalmist gives a beautiful description of how God stills the storms in the lives of His children. He guarantees their safety on the stormy seas of life. They are assured that they will arrive safely at their destination, because He is with them.

When God is the captain of our ship, we can know for certain that He will guide us safely to the harbor where we long to be: heaven that He Himself has prepared for His children.

*Lord, no matter how bad the storms in my life get, I know that
I can turn to You and You will still them for me. Amen.*

GOD'S FLYING LESSONS

He shielded him and cared for him; he guarded him as the apple of his eye, like an eagle that stirs up its nest and hovers over its young, that spreads its wings to catch them and carries them on its pinions. The LORD alone led him.

DEUTERONOMY 32:10-12

Eagles kick their young out of the nest when they think the babies are big enough to fly. This is not a very pleasant experience for the young eaglets, but it is necessary for them to test their wings. The parent eagles, however, hover near to ensure that the babies come to no harm.

God longs for you to reach spiritual maturity. That is why He sometimes pushes you out of the nest of your daily routine. When you encounter crises and problems, then God is teaching you how to fly!

Father, I realize that the challenges I face today might be my first flying lesson. Stay with me, Lord, so that I will not fall.

Amen.

GOD FORGIVES

You will again have compassion on us;
you will tread our sins underfoot and hurl
all our iniquities into the depths of the sea.

MICAH 7:19

God is merciful. Not only does He not hold our sins against us, not only is He prepared to forgive us our sins, but He casts our sins into the sea of forgetfulness. He throws them into the deep blue sea, and never thinks of them again. And He asks us to do the same.

Forgiving is easier than forgetting. God is prepared to forget your sins, therefore you should be prepared to forgive people who sin against you in the same way. Are you nurturing a grudge against anyone? It's time to forget about it.

Father God, help me to forgive others the way You forgive me. Remove all hatred and vengefulness from my heart, and replace it with Your love and mercy. Amen.

May 20

SINFULNESS

For all have sinned and fall short of the glory of God, and are justified freely by his grace through the redemption that came by Christ Jesus.

ROMANS 3:23-24

Each person on earth is born a sinner. We do not naturally want to live close to God. But the good news is that He loves us so much that He would not leave us in our sinfulness. Through His grace He sets us free, because the death of Jesus on the cross paid the price for our sins.

Jesus offers reconciliation to you in place of the burden of your sin. You can never earn His grace. All you need to do to make it yours is to believe in Him.

Lord Jesus, I believe in You as my Lord and Savior. Because of Your sacrifice, I am reconciled to God and have a future in heaven. Thank You, Lord. Amen.

GOD WANTS TO USE YOU

Brothers, each man, as responsible to God,
should remain in the situation God called him to.

1 CORINTHIANS 7:24

You might sometimes think that you would be able to serve God more effectively in a different place: on the mission field, or in a different town or city. But God has different ideas. He is the One who placed you, and your family, where you are, in your town, in your street, in your community.

God desires to use you to serve Him where you are right now. Begin to serve Him today, and don't keep yearning for different circumstances.

Lord, here I am. Open my eyes to how I can serve You right here, right now. Amen.

HE HAS GIVEN YOU ALL THAT YOU NEED

"Bring the whole tithe into the storehouse, that there may be food in my house. Test me in this," says the LORD *Almighty, "and see if I will not throw open the floodgates of heaven and pour out so much blessing that you will not have room enough for it."*

MALACHI 3:10

*M*alachi challenged the people to test God: if they were prepared to give Him the portion that He asked of them, He would undertake to care for them and bless them, far beyond what they could ever have imagined.

Are you prepared to accept the same challenge? God is always faithful to the promises in His Word. Give God the part of your income that rightly belongs to Him – and He will make sure that you have everything that you need – in abundance.

Lord, I give to You what is Yours. Thank You for Your promise of provision and blessing. Amen.

DON'T GO TO
BED ANGRY

*"In your anger do not sin": Do not let the
sun go down while you are still angry.*

EPHESIANS 4:26

It is very hard to fall asleep when you are extremely angry with someone else. Therefore, don't nurture your anger and hold it over till the next day. If you are unhappy, talk about it and clear the unpleasantness from the air, and then it will not be necessary to end your day with anger.

Restrain your temper. Don't ever go to bed angry. Make sure that all misunderstandings have been cleared up before the day is over.

Lord Jesus, remove any anger and bitterness from my heart. Help me to clear up any misunderstandings or feelings of unhappiness before the day is done. Amen.

LISTEN TO OTHER PEOPLE

There is a time for everything, and a season for every activity under heaven: ... a time to tear and a time to mend, a time to be silent and a time to speak.

ECCLESIASTES 3:1, 7

It is unfortunate that so few people know this simple secret: there is a time to talk and a time to be silent. We usually can't wait to voice our own opinions, and so we listen impatiently to the opinions and ideas of others.

Communication involves both talking and listening. And communication is very important. Remember that there is a time when it is necessary for you to remain silent. Be prepared to listen to others' points of view before you air your own opinion.

Father, help me to become better at communicating, to listen patiently, to think before I speak and to know when to keep quiet. Amen.

YOU ARE UNIQUE

I praise you because I am fearfully and wonderfully made; your works are wonderful, I know that full well.

PSALM 139:14

*E*ach person is a small miracle. The more science discovers about the human body, the more clearly we realize this. If you haven't yet been struck by the awesome way in which God made us, just do a few internet searches on how the body works.

Never again will you feel unworthy. You are unique. God has made you in a wonderful way. In this world with its billions of people, there is only one you! You can be proud of the fact that God has made you so special.

Creator God, You made me in Your own image, sculpted me to be unique and beautiful. Thank You for putting so much care and thought and love into the sculpting of me.

Amen.

NEGATIVE THOUGHTS

*Above all else, guard your heart,
for it is the wellspring of life.*

PROVERBS 4:23

Be careful of what you think. The way you think has a deep impact on your whole life. You are what you think! What your heart is filled with will ultimately determine the course of your life, says the writer of Proverbs.

If you think negative thoughts all day long, your whole outlook on life will become negative and you will have a negative influence on others too.

Teach yourself to think positive thoughts so that your life can be filled with light and joy.

Lord, I want to shine Your light, Your love, for all to see. Work in me, Lord, and change my thoughts. Fill me with Your positive light so that I can radiate Your joy and love. Amen.

GIVE YOURSELF TO GOD

Therefore, I urge you, brothers, in view of God's mercy, to offer your bodies as living sacrifices, holy and pleasing to God – this is your spiritual act of worship.

ROMANS 12:1

*B*elievers should be prepared to surrender their whole life to God, to be living sacrifices that God will gladly receive. This is the essence of what serving God is all about.

If you want your spiritual life to be meaningful to yourself and others, you need to be prepared to give everything you have – including yourself – to God. Live so that you serve Him with every part of your life.

I want to serve You with all of my being, Lord. I give You everything I have, my entire being. Let Your will be done.

Amen.

JESUS TRIUMPHED OVER DEATH

And if Christ has not been raised,
our preaching is useless and so is your faith.

1 CORINTHIANS 15:14

*P*aul declared that if Jesus did not rise from the dead, everything that he preached was meaningless and the faith of the Corinthians was groundless. Then they were still living in their sin, explained Paul in his letter.

But Jesus conquered death. He rose from the dead and lives forevermore so that you will be able to live with Him forever. That is why you need no longer live in sin, but can accept the salvation Jesus offers. You don't have to fear death; you are victorious in faith.

Thank You, Jesus, for conquering death so that I may receive the promise of eternal life with You in heaven. Amen.

JESUS WILL COME AGAIN

"Men of Galilee," they said, "why do you stand here looking into the sky? This same Jesus, who has been taken from you into heaven, will come back in the same way you have seen him go into heaven."

ACTS 1:11

*J*ust after Jesus ascended to heaven, two men in white clothes told the group of astounded disciples who were staring up into the sky that Jesus would come again. He would return to His disciples in exactly the same way in which He went to His Father.

This promise is still valid for us today. Jesus will come again in glory – and all people will see Him. This will be a joyful event that you can anticipate with real hope.

Lord, I look forward to the day You will return to earth in Your glorious light, taking up Your children to live with You forever in heaven. Amen.

NO ONE KNOWS

He who testifies to these things says, "Yes, I am coming soon." Amen. Come, Lord Jesus.

REVELATION 22:20

That Jesus will return is an undeniable fact, but when it will happen, no one knows, not even Jesus Himself. Only the Father knows when Jesus will return. And He is merciful. He is holding off the Second Coming of Christ until everyone has a chance to respond to His gift of grace.

You will see Jesus soon, if not at His Second Coming, then on the day you die. And not one of us knows when that will be. Live as if you expect Him every day.

Lord Jesus, help me to live every day as though it were my last day. Send Your Spirit to work in me and change me so that I will be ready when You come again. Amen.

AN INSTRUMENT OF GOD'S PEACE

*Surely his salvation is near those who fear him,
that his glory may dwell in our land.*

PSALM 85:9

God desires that everyone who believes in Him have peace. But there is a condition to this promise of peace: they need to be prepared to serve Him and obey Him in all things He asks of them.

God offers His peace to you. If every Christian in the world is prepared to listen to God and to become an instrument of His peace, imagine how wonderful the world would be.

Father, make me an instrument of Your peace. Let me sow Your seed of peace in a dark and barren world. Amen.

June

YOUR FATHER IS ALWAYS NEAR

"I am the vine; you are the branches. If a man remains in me and I in him, he will bear much fruit; apart from me you can do nothing."

JOHN 15:5

Without the vine, the branches cannot even attempt to bear bunches of grapes. It is a physical impossibility. In the same way, the children of God cannot even try to bear fruit without God – it just cannot be done. But when we abide in Him, the fruit comes naturally.

You do not need to struggle on your own to get things right – your Father is always with you to help you. Without Him you can do nothing, but in His strength there is nothing that you cannot do.

Heavenly Father, I realize more and more each day that without You, I am nothing. Without You, I can do nothing. Never let me be cut off from You, Lord. Amen.

A PURPOSE IN EVERY CRISIS

And we know that in all things God works for the good of those who love him, who have been called according to his purpose. No, in all these things we are more than conquerors through him who loved us.

ROMANS 8:28, 37

It is unfortunately true that bad things often happen to good people. Things that are beyond our ability to explain rationally, and that are hard to reconcile with God's love. In such crises, we can hold on to the truth that God causes all things to work together for our good.

Everything that happens to you is ultimately for your own good because God has a purpose with each crisis that He allows to come your way. In His strength you can always be more than a conqueror.

Father God, in any crisis I can have hope, because You have promised to take care of me. I know that everything will work out for the best, because You are with me. Amen.

WISDOM AND INSIGHT

They will still bear fruit in old age,
they will stay fresh and green.

PSALM 92:14

*P*eople today are living longer than ever before. We are only just beginning to realize how much old people can contribute to society with the wisdom and insight and experience that they have gained over the years.

But getting older can also bring many negative things, and that is why we find it hard to come to terms with growing old. When a person gets old, you are not less valuable to God. You can use the wisdom and insight that life has given you to increase your worth and value.

Father, help me to see growing older not as a thing to be feared, but rather as a testimony of a life well lived. *Amen.*

CONFESS YOUR OWN SIN

I confess my iniquity; I am troubled by my sin.

PSALM 38:18

*T*he Bible tells us over and over again that it does not pay to try to hide our sins from God. It is of course impossible to do so, because He knows everything about us anyway.

Ask Him to make you sensitive to the wrong things in your life that constantly plague you. Confess them one by one so that God can forgive you for them.

When relationships have gone wrong you need to confess your own sin before men and before God. Always be ready to be the first one to say that you're sorry.

Lord, open my eyes to the sins I've committed so that I may repent. Let me never be too proud or too stubborn to admit when I've sinned and ask for forgiveness. Amen.

BELIEVE THAT GOD KNOWS BEST

"For my thoughts are not your thoughts, neither are your ways my ways," declares the LORD. "As the heavens are higher than the earth, so are my ways higher than your ways and my thoughts than your thoughts."

ISAIAH 55:8-9

God thinks and acts in ways that are completely different from the way we think and act. He always knows best, even if we cannot understand the way in which He does things.

God is incomparably great and wonderful. Everything He does He does for your own good. It isn't necessary for you to understand everything He does – simply believe that He knows best.

Father, I do not always understand Your ways, but I trust in You. I know that You have only my best interests at heart.

Amen.

RESIST THE DEVIL

*Be self-controlled and alert. Your enemy the
devil prowls around like a roaring lion looking for
someone to devour. Resist him, standing firm in the faith,
because you know that your brothers throughout the
world are undergoing the same kind of sufferings.*

1 PETER 5:8-9

*E*ven though some people think that the devil doesn't exist, he is very much alive and he is stronger than you. But God gives you the weapons that you can use to overcome him. And Jesus conquered him on the cross.

You can do nothing to withstand the devil in your own strength. He is stronger than you, but in God's strength you can resist him and come out of the fray as the victor.

Lord, I cannot withstand the devil's attacks in my own strength. I need Your help, Lord, to keep the devil at bay.

Amen.

FORGIVE OTHERS

"For if you forgive men when they sin against you,
your heavenly Father will also forgive you."

MATTHEW 6:14

*J*esus told His disciples that God would forgive them if they forgave others. If we understand the worth of God's forgiveness of us we will be prepared to forgive others. But it still remains difficult to keep forgiving someone who continuously makes us angry.

Love cannot be measured. Don't try to count how many times you have forgiven someone. Be prepared to forgive them every time, as God does with you.

Heavenly Father, forgiveness does not come easy for me, especially when I don't feel the person deserves it. Give me Your heart of mercy and forgiveness. Help me to forgive others like You forgive me. Amen.

June 8

BE CAREFUL
WHAT YOU SAY

*I said, "I will watch my ways and keep my
tongue from sin; I will put a muzzle on my mouth
as long as the wicked are in my presence."*

PSALM 39:1

Many of us harm others by the things that we thoughtlessly say about them. Before you say something about someone else, consider that you can never take back the words that you speak. What's been said has been said.

Our sharp words can wound another person. Children of the Lord must try to set a guard before their mouths at all times. Think very carefully before you blurt something out that you will later regret.

Father, put a guard on my mouth. Do not let me speak words that are meant to break down or discourage. Amen.

YOU SHOULD BE A LIGHT-BEARER

"You are the light of the world. A city on a hill cannot be hidden. ... In the same way, let your light shine before men, that they may see your good deeds and praise your Father in heaven."

MATTHEW 5:14, 16

Jesus proclaimed that He is the light of the world. But His children are also lights – lights that shine before other people so that they can see the good things we do and so glorify our heavenly Father.

As a planet reflects the light of the sun, God wants us to bear His light in this world. When people look at you, they should see Jesus in the things that you do and say.

Lord, I want to be a light for You. Help me to live in such a way that others will see You in me and want to know You too. Amen.

FOLLOW HIS PATH

"I will instruct you and teach you in the way you should go; I will counsel you and watch over you."

PSALM 32:8

God offers to guide His children: He wants to teach them and show them the right road. He wants to counsel us when we need advice, and He watches over us all the time.

God loves you so much that He knows exactly where you are at the moment, and what you are busy doing. You can always get help and counsel from Him. He watches over you and directs you on the path you should follow.

Father, guide me on the right path, in the way You want me to go. Amen.

THE BEST RESPONSE TO GOD

Give thanks to the LORD, for he is good;
his love endures forever.

PSALM 107:1

*G*od's children experience His goodness and mercy every day. When you pause and consider God's overwhelming love and mercy for you, you will not be able to stop yourself from singing praises to Him.

The best response that you can give God for His goodness to you is to sing a song of praise to Him. Don't ever stop praising Him!

God, I praise You for Your goodness to me. There is no other god like You. All the might and the glory and the honor belong to You. Amen.

FAITH IS ESSENTIAL

"Have faith in God," Jesus answered. "I tell you the truth, if anyone says to this mountain, 'Go, throw yourself into the sea,' and does not doubt in his heart but believes that what he says will happen, it will be done for him."

MARK 11:22-23

*F*aith can perform wonders. But faith is not to be used to try to manipulate God for the things we selfishly desire. When we pray, we must believe that God will give us those things that we ask of Him, as long as they are in His will.

Faith should be the Christian's steering wheel, and not the spare wheel. It is an essential part of your life that should not just be used in emergencies.

Father, I long to know You better. Help me to grow daily in my understanding of You so that my faith may also grow stronger. Amen.

June 13

A GOD OF MIRACLES

Then Jesus said, "Did I not tell you that if you
believed, you would see the glory of God?"

JOHN 11:40

*T*he sisters of Lazarus, and all the others who were present, were speechless when Jesus raised Lazarus from the
dead. It seemed completely impossible. But God is almighty. He can do the impossible. And He is still able to
perform miracles.

God's words are true for us too. If we believe, we will
see the demonstration of His power. If you believe, you
will discover that God is a God of miracles. Nothing is
impossible for Him.

Almighty Father, You are a miracle-working God. Nothing is
impossible for You. I stand in awe of You. Amen.

CHRISTIANS ALWAYS WIN

I can do everything through him who gives me strength.

PHILIPPIANS 4:13

*P*aul was able to achieve wonderful things because God was his source of strength. And God's strength is just as available to us as it was to Paul.

We too can draw on His strength when we encounter crises in our lives. Over and over we find that we can do all things because God gives us His strength. God makes His miracle-working power available to all His children.

If you are facing difficult situations, you can be on the winning side if you know where your strength comes from. There is nothing that you and God cannot achieve together.

With You by my side, Lord, nothing is impossible. No obstacle will be too big to overcome, no battle unconquerable, as long as I have You. Amen.

SHOW YOUR LOVE

*Dear children, let us not love with words
or tongue but with actions and in truth.*

1 JOHN 3:18

Words do not mean much unless you are prepared to put action to your promises. This is also true of our love for God, says John. We need to show our love by the things that we do, and these acts of love need to be sincere too.

If you realize the extent of God's love for you, and how much it cost Him to bring His love to you, you would be compelled to show your love for Him through your actions.

Father, I know that words don't amount to much without actions, so I promise to show my love for You in the way I choose to live. Amen.

GOD WILL NEVER LET YOU DOWN

I will lie down and sleep in peace,
for you alone, O Lord, make me dwell in safety.

PSALM 4:8

Christians have a deep sense of peace that other people find hard to understand. Because we know that God loves us, we also know that God promises to protect us, that He will never disappoint us, and that we are assured of His presence each day. Therefore, we do not need to lie awake at night worrying.

You can live joyfully each day and sleep peacefully each night because God will never let you down.

Lord, every night I go to bed knowing that You are with me. And every morning I rise knowing that You are waiting to greet me. Thank You for Your constant presence in my life.

Amen.

GOD IS THERE FOR HIS CHILDREN

For he wounds, but he also binds up; he injures, but his hands also heal. From six calamities he will rescue you; in seven no harm will befall you.

JOB 5:18-19

*J*ob knew in his heart that he would not always be able to protect his children from disasters and trouble. He literally lost everything, except his faith in the God who was testing him. Eliphas, his friend, assured him that God would bind up his wounds and would ultimately deliver him.

Sometimes God allows disasters to strike His children, but He is always there to help them when they ask Him for His help.

Father, I am going through troublesome times. Please help me. Rescue me. Amen.

GRACE IS A FREE GIFT

*It does not, therefore, depend on man's
desire or effort, but on God's mercy.*

ROMANS 9:16

God's decision to adopt people as His children is not dependent on anything that we do or don't do. He calls people to Himself because of His grace. And He owes us nothing. He shows mercy to those whom He chooses.

You cannot do anything that will influence Him in His decision. If you accept His offer of mercy, you should never stop thanking Him for His grace toward you.

Thank You, Father God, for Your loving mercy. I praise You for Your compassion, love and grace. Amen.

SINCERE SYMPATHY

Then Job replied: "Listen carefully to my words;
let this be the consolation you give me."

JOB 21:1-2

*J*ob was deeply appreciative of the sympathy his three friends showed him by sitting silently with him for a whole week while he was suffering his traumatic losses. But when they began to talk to him, their words upset him horribly.

Sometimes we do not know what to say to someone who is going through difficult times. A hug and sincere sympathy for someone who is facing problems is far better comfort than a string of meaningless words.

Father, help me to realize when it is necessary to comfort with words and when my presence is more than enough.

Amen.

June 20

NO ONE KNOWS
THE FUTURE

*To them God has chosen to make known
among the Gentiles the glorious riches of this
mystery, which is Christ in you, the hope of glory.*

COLOSSIANS 1:27

In the New Testament, God reveals the secret that He had hinted at in the Old Testament: Jesus makes heaven accessible to all of us, even those people who do not belong to God's special nation. If you believe in Him, He comes to live in you. He is your hope for the future.

Not one of us knows just what the future holds, but if we know Jesus, we are assured that He will be present in our future. He is our only hope for reaching the heaven that we long for.

Lord, You are my only hope of heaven. Guide me through the narrow gate so that I might make Your promise of eternal life my own (see Mt. 7:13). Amen.

GOD SETS YOU FREE

*But now that you have been set free from sin
and have become slaves to God, the benefit you
reap leads to holiness, and the result is eternal life.*

ROMANS 6:22

To live in sin is a dead-end street. But God sets us free from our sins and takes us into His service. He guarantees that we will have eternal life. But the responsibility to be the kind of person that God wants us to be lies with us.

If God has set you free from your sins, you should use your new freedom to serve Him and to live a holy life. Then you will be assured of eternal life.

Father, help me to be the person You created me to be.

Amen.

SPIRITUAL GROWTH

*You do not have, because you do not ask
God. … Come near to God and he will come
near to you. Wash your hands, you sinners,
and purify your hearts, you double-minded.*

JAMES 4:2, 8

Although many people pray, they do not often receive answers to their prayers, because they live far from God. People who love God and live close to Him find that God draws near to them and He gives them the things that they ask for.

Prayer is the thermometer that measures the spiritual growth and strength of Christians. What does your prayer life look like? If you stay close to God, He will hear your prayers and help you become spiritually stronger day by day.

Heavenly Father, draw me closer to You every day. I want to have an intimate relationship with You and get to know You more and more. Amen.

June 23

HE CONTROLS
YOUR LIFE

*But just as he who called you is holy,
so be holy in all you do.*

1 PETER 1:15

*T*he same God who calls us to be His children is holy and without sin. And He expects us to have nothing to do with sin.

Ask Him to show you the things in your life that are sinful and to help you to get rid of them once and for all, so that you can become more like Jesus.

If you allow the Holy Spirit to take control of your life, God can turn a sinful human being into a saint.

Lord Jesus, show me what is sinful in my life so that I can turn away from it once and for all, and become more like You.

Amen.

PRAYER IS A CONVERSATION

*"Ask and it will be given to you; seek and you
will find; knock and the door will be opened to you."*

MATTHEW 7:7

God's children should never grow tired of praying. What we ask for in prayer, God promises to do. We never walk away from God empty-handed. That is why we feel so much better when we have laid our desires at the feet of God.

Prayer is a conversation between two people who love each other. When you pray, God gives you what you ask for, providing that it is within His will.

Father, I lay my desires, my needs, my cares, before You. I trust You to take care of me and to give me only what is best for me. Amen.

GOD KNOWS
YOUR NEEDS

*"... for your Father knows what you
need before you ask him."*

MATTHEW 6:8

*I*t is not necessary to pray long-winded prayers in which you list each of your requests to God. This was what Jesus told His disciples when they asked Him to teach them to pray.

God knows us so well that He already knows exactly what our needs are long before we put them into words. God knows you personally and intimately and He knows each one of your needs. He knows exactly what you need before you ask Him.

Father, You know better than anyone what my needs are right now. I give my life into Your hand. Let Your will be done.

Amen.

GOD GIVES
YOU STRENGTH

*Three times I pleaded with the Lord to take it away
from me. But he said to me, "My grace is sufficient
for you, for my power is made perfect in weakness."
Therefore I will boast all the more gladly about my
weaknesses, so that Christ's power may rest on me.*

2 CORINTHIANS 12:8-9

*P*aul prayed earnestly that God would remove the
thorn that hindered him, but God did not answer his
prayer. He wanted Paul to learn that His power works
most effectively when His children are weak. His grace is
sufficient for us.

Sometimes God does not change your circumstances,
but He always gives you the strength to work through
your situation in a positive way. And when you are weak,
His strength is at its most effective.

*Lord, Your grace is all I need, because when I am weak, You
are strong. Amen.*

LEARN TO PRAY
BY PRAYING

One day Jesus was praying in a certain place. When he finished, one of his disciples said to him, "Lord, teach us to pray, just as John taught his disciples."

LUKE 11:1

The disciples of Jesus saw how much joy and strength He derived from the fellowship of prayer He enjoyed with the Father. That is why they asked Him to teach them to pray.

Perhaps you have wished that Jesus could teach you to pray. All that you need to do if you desire to talk to God is simply to talk to Him. Tell God what is in your heart. Just as we learned to write by practicing writing, we learn to pray by praying.

Father God, most days I don't know what to pray. But that doesn't mean that I don't want to talk to You. Teach me to pray even when I don't know what to say. Amen.

A SONG OF PRAISE

*Let everything that has breath
praise the LORD. Praise the LORD.*

PSALM 150:6

*T*he whole of Psalm 150 is an exuberant song of praise to God. The psalmist invites everyone to join him in his song of praise and to praise God for who He is. God deserves to be praised with every kind of musical instrument imaginable by everyone who has breath.

When you are feeling depressed and discouraged, sing a song of praise to God. Praise Him in every possible way. You will find that your heaviness will dissipate like the mist before the sun.

I praise You, Lord, for the wonderful joy that comes with knowing You. Amen.

HIS PERFECT WILL

"Not everyone who says to me, 'Lord, Lord,' will enter the kingdom of heaven, but only he who does the will of my Father who is in heaven."

MATTHEW 7:21

These words of Jesus leave us with an uneasy feeling: only those people who do what He says will find a place in His new kingdom. Getting to heaven requires more from you than just saying the right words. You also need to be prepared to be obedient to God.

Are you prepared to submit your own desires to God's will? Only when His perfect will rules in your life will you be completely happy.

Father, let Your perfect will rule in my life. I am ready to die to self, pick up my cross and follow You. Amen.

SEEK GOD'S
KINGDOM FIRST

*"But seek first his kingdom and his righteousness,
and all these things will be given to you as well."*

MATTHEW 6:33

$\mathcal{D}$o the things that are important to God, be obedient to His will, ensure that His Kingdom grows, and He will take care of all the other things in your life. This is what Jesus promises in the Sermon on the Mount.

God provides for each one of His children's needs. We do not need to worry about tomorrow because He will care for us in the future as well.

If you are prepared to put God's Kingdom first, He will meet each one of your needs.

Father God, I want to be obedient to You. Help me to always put Your will, Your Kingdom, first before anything else.

$\mathcal{A}men.$

July

GOD IS WITH YOU ALL DAY

Pray continually.

1 THESSALONIANS 5:17

It is a good idea to write in your diary a specific time every day to spend with God. But you can also speak to God at any time during the day – not just during the time set aside for your devotions. God is always ready to listen to what you have to say.

Try to pray at different moments during the day: when you are waiting for the traffic lights to change, when you are in a supermarket queue, while you're preparing supper, at the post office, at work ... in this way you will be aware that God is with you throughout the entire day.

Thank You, Father, that I can talk to You wherever I am. No place is off limits and no time is inconvenient for You.

Amen.

A WAY OF LIFE

"But when you pray, go into your room, close the door and pray to your Father, who is unseen. Then your Father, who sees what is done in secret, will reward you."

MATTHEW 6:6

God wants continuous and faithful communication with Him to be an integral part of His children's lives. Can you imagine what your life would be like if you never talked to God?

Set aside time each day to be alone with God. The busier your day is, the more you need your quiet time. Talk to God about everything in your life. In this way prayer will become a way of life for you.

Lord, help me to make prayer such an integral part of my life that it later becomes second nature to me. Amen.

GOD KNOWS YOU

Your eyes saw my unformed body. All the days ordained for me were written in your book before one of them came to be.

PSALM 139:16

The psalmist is in awe by the fact that God knows him so well, that He knew him even before he was born, that God had already planned each day of his life.

God knows you just as thoroughly. He knew you before you were born, too. He knows exactly what each day of your life will be like. You can hide nothing from Him. And simply because God knows you so well, you can trust Him completely.

Father, You know every little atom of my being. You alone know what my future holds. Therefore I place my trust in You.

Amen.

GOD GIVES ABUNDANTLY

I am the LORD your God, who brought you up out of Egypt. Open wide your mouth and I will fill it.

PSALM 81:10

God reassures His people over and over again that He will care for them because He is their God. He promises not only to give them the things that they need, but also that He will give far more than what is needed. And He honors His word.

If you belong to God, He makes this promise to you, too. God is with you every day and He will take good care of you. He never does things in half-measures; He gives abundantly.

Father God, Your generosity knows no bounds. Your abundant blessings are far better than we could ever hope for. Thank You! Amen.

THE GOOD NEWS
OF GOD'S LOVE

I am obligated both to Greeks and non-Greeks, both to the wise and the foolish. That is why I am so eager to preach the gospel also to you who are at Rome.

ROMANS 1:14-15

The love of God compelled Paul to tell as many people as he could the good news of Jesus. He longed to minister the gospel to people in Rome so that those who had never before heard about Jesus could also be saved.

The grace of God makes you into a debtor: you owe people around you the good news of God's love. You should never be ashamed to witness for Him.

May Your Spirit, Lord, turn me into a powerful witness for You. Amen.

THE SINCERITY OF YOUR LOVE

*I am not commanding you, but I want to
test the sincerity of your love by comparing
it with the earnestness of others.*

2 CORINTHIANS 8:8

Paul told the Corinthians that the way you treat less fortunate people shows whether your love for the Lord is genuine or mere lip service. He went on to tell them how committed other Christians are to supporting and assisting the needy.

The sincerity of your love for the Lord is still measured by what you are prepared to offer His Kingdom. What do you do for people who have less than you do?

Father, there are so many people out there who have less than I do. Give me a heart for them and show me what I can do to help them. Amen.

LIVE FOR JESUS

*In the same way, count yourselves dead
to sin but alive to God in Christ Jesus.*

ROMANS 6:11

Sin no longer has a hold on God's children. The sinful nature with which they were born no longer holds sway in their lives. They are dead to sin. They should now live for God because they have been made one with Christ.

To be holy means that once you are born again you reckon yourself as dead to sin and alive to Jesus. Are you prepared to live for Jesus?

Lord Jesus, I want to live for You. I am ready to pick up my cross and follow You. Amen.

July 8

LIVE IN HOLINESS

Do not offer the parts of your body to sin, as instruments of wickedness, but rather offer yourselves to God, as those who have been brought from death to life; and offer the parts of your body to him as instruments of righteousness. For sin shall not be your master, because you are not under law, but under grace.

ROMANS 6:13-14

Christians should be careful never to yield any part of their body to sin. They should be completely committed to God. Every part of their lives should be dedicated to God and to doing the things that He asks them in His Word to do.

If you are willing to offer every part of your body to the service of God then He will help you to live a holy life.

Father, I lay my life before You. Please send Your Spirit to live in me and to guide me in living a holy life. *Amen.*

TRUST GOD

*As the Scripture says, "Anyone who trusts
in him will never be put to shame."*

ROMANS 10:11

When you work with people, you very quickly discover that few people are really trustworthy. People are not perfect, and so it is inevitable that at one time or another someone will let you down. The trust that you have placed in them will be broken.

But God is different. If you believe in God and trust Him, you can be sure of one thing: He will never disappoint you.

Lord, even though I cannot always trust people, I know that I can always trust You. You are a faithful God who will keep Your promises. Amen.

ETERNAL LIFE

*Jesus said to her, "I am the resurrection
and the life. He who believes in me will live,
even though he dies; and whoever lives and
believes in me will never die. Do you believe this?"*

JOHN 11:25-26

When Martha asked Jesus why He had not prevented her brother from dying, He explained that He is the resurrection and the life: the one who raises people from the dead and gives them a life that never ends.

Everyone who believes in Jesus is assured of eternal life. When Jesus died on the cross He made it possible for you to live forever. That is why you can already have the assurance that you have eternal life.

Jesus, there are no words for the gratitude I feel for what You did for me when You died on the cross. Thank You, Lord.

Amen.

July 11

FAITH ALWAYS
PRODUCES RESULTS

He replied, "If you have faith as small as a mustard seed, you can say to this mulberry tree, 'Be uprooted and planted in the sea,' and it will obey you."

LUKE 17:6

All that is needed to make the impossible possible is faith as small as a mustard seed, the smallest of all seeds, so said Jesus to His disciples.

Even if your faith is very small, God is ready to listen to you. God responds to the requests His children make. Faith is calling out to God. Faith will not be silenced, and faith always produces results.

Father, when I look at other believers, I often feel that I'm lacking in the faith department. But that's not true. Even faith as small as a mustard seed is enough for You. Amen.

GOD PROMISES YOU HIS JOY

Make us glad for as many days as you have afflicted us, for as many years as we have seen trouble.

PSALM 90:15

The psalmist prays that God will give Him as many days of joy as the days of heaviness that he has endured.

God's children need never live without hope, no matter how bad things seem. They are assured of a happy ending, of eternity in heaven together with God.

Your trials and tribulations on earth endure only for a short while. And then the difficult times will end and God promises that you will have joy forevermore.

Father, I can endure the difficult times right now because I know that one day they will come to an end. I believe in Your promise of eternal life. Amen.

YOU ARE THE CHURCH OF GOD

*Now you are the body of Christ,
and each one of you is a part of it.*

1 CORINTHIANS 12:27

*W*e won't always be happy with every single decision that is made in our church. We find it easy to criticize and might even decide not to go to church anymore. But who is actually the church? Not the congregation or the building. The church of God is made up of individuals – just like you.

Next time you feel like criticizing your church, remember that you are part of the community of God, the church of God upon this earth. Therefore, if you really want to see things change, start with yourself.

Lord, help me to focus on my own weaknesses rather than criticizing others. Amen.

USE YOUR GIFTS

Now to each one the manifestation of the Spirit is given for the common good. All these are the work of one and the same Spirit, and he gives them to each one, just as he determines.

1 CORINTHIANS 12:7, 11

*T*he Holy Spirit works in a unique way in each of God's children. God has given each one of us gifts that we can use to serve others. But sadly we are so inclined to compare our gifts with what other people can do that we end up neglecting our own.

Each of us has different kinds of gifts, and giftings in different degrees. But God has given each one of us specific gifts with which we can glorify Him and that should be used in His service. Use the gifts He has given you to honor Him.

Father God, help me to appreciate my gifts, and use them in service of others. Amen.

FOLLOW JESUS

Then he called the crowd to him along with his disciples and said: "If anyone would come after me, he must deny himself and take up his cross and follow me."

MARK 8:34

*J*esus is never satisfied with half measures. If you follow Him you must be prepared to take second place, to leave everything behind you, to give your whole life to Him, even to endure hard times and yet serve Him.

It is worthwhile to forsake all things and follow Jesus. The joy that disciples experience is far greater than the pain of any demands that might be made on you.

Lord Jesus, I give my life to You. Here I am. I am ready to take up my cross, place myself last and follow You. Amen.

July 16

YOUR POSSESSIONS

*Jesus looked at him and loved him. "One thing
you lack," he said. "Go, sell everything you have and
give to the poor, and you will have treasure in heaven.
Then come, follow me." At this the man's face fell.
He went away sad, because he had great wealth.*

MARK 10:21-22

It might seem that Jesus set an excessively difficult task on the rich young man. How many of us would really be prepared to sell all our possessions, give the proceeds to the poor in order to "lay up treasures in heaven"?

Jesus does not expect you to get rid of all your assets. When your possessions become a higher priority in your life than your relationship with God, you should hear a warning bell ringing in your heart.

Lord, I don't want my possessions to become the most important thing in my life. Help me to remain focused on You and Your will for my life. Amen.

HE CHOSE YOU

For he chose us in him before the creation of the world to be holy and blameless in his sight.

EPHESIANS 1:4

People have different opinions on the concept of pre-destination. Some think that it is unfair that there are many people who will never be given the chance to make a decision to serve God. Even before the creation of the world God knew who His children would be.

You do not need to tire yourself out trying to under-stand predestination. God decides in His mercy who His children will be. If you hear His voice and respond to it, you will know that He has chosen you.

Thank You, Lord, for choosing me. Thank You for adopting me as Your child. Amen.

WHEN WE MEET GOD

"God did this so that men would seek him and perhaps reach out for him and find him, though he is not far from each one of us. 'For in him we live and move and have our being.' As some of your own poets have said, 'We are his offspring.'"

ACTS 17:27-28

We all long for peace. One of the early church fathers, Augustine, wrote a prayer that has become very famous: "Thou hast made us for Thyself, O Lord; and our heart is restless until it rests in Thee."

God created people with a desire to seek Him. There is a longing in each one of us that can only be stilled when we meet God. Don't stop looking until you find God.

Lord, I long to be in Your presence. Don't hide from me. Draw me closer and closer to You every day. Amen.

EYES OF LOVE

My brothers, as believers in our glorious
Lord Jesus Christ, don't show favoritism.

JAMES 2:1

When we talk about other people, we tend to criticize or judge them according to our limited understanding of their lives and circumstances: what they look like, where they live, what work they do and what kind of car they drive. We seem to think that rich and popular people are much more important than ordinary, average people.

God never looks at people in terms of dollars and cents, but through eyes of love. Guard against judging people on outward appearances. Rather look at them through the eyes of God's love.

Father, help me to see people through Your eyes of love.

Amen.

IN GOD'S SERVICE

Whatever your hand finds to do, do it with all your might, for in the grave, where you are going, there is neither working nor planning nor knowledge nor wisdom.

ECCLESIASTES 9:10

*N*o one knows how long they will live. That is why we should diligently put our hand to the tasks before us.

Do not be lazy. Be prepared to do your part in the Kingdom of God. If you are prepared to give your strength, talents and time in God's service, you will find that your life here on earth will be good preparation for your life in heaven.

Father, here I am, ready to serve. Everything I do, I promise to do to the best of my abilities and to Your glory. Amen.

BE AVAILABLE

And he has given us this command: Whoever loves God must also love his brother. Everyone who believes that Jesus is the Christ is born of God, and everyone who loves the father loves his child as well.

1 JOHN 4:21-5:1

*I*f we love God, we should also love other people. God expects this of His children: each one who loves Him should love his fellow believers too. John says that if you do not love people whom you can see, then you do not love God whom you cannot see.

God showed how much He loves you by letting His Son die in your place. You should show your love for Him by loving other people and being available to help them.

Heavenly Father, help me to love others, whether I like them or not, and to help them as best I can. Amen.

BE SENSITIVE TO THE NEEDS OF OTHERS

*Our desire is not that others might be relieved
while you are hard pressed, but that there might be
equality. At the present time your plenty will supply
what they need, so that in turn their plenty will
supply what you need. Then there will be equality.*

2 CORINTHIANS 8:13-14

*P*aul writes to the Corinthians that he does not expect them to give so much to others that they will themselves lack what they need. But those people who have more than enough should be prepared to help those who do not have enough.

There are many people around you who go to sleep hungry at night. We should all help the poor and needy as far as we are able.

*Father, open my eyes to the needs of others so that I can share
my blessings with them. Amen.*

THE LORD REQUIRES YOUR WILLINGNESS

*For it is God who works in you to will
and to act according to his good purpose.*

PHILIPPIANS 2:13

We can't achieve anything in our own strength – especially regarding the work we do in God's Kingdom.

God promises to equip us and make us willing to do the things that He requires of us and so fulfill His purpose. All we need to do is report for duty.

The Lord does not expect you to be highly competent before He will use you in His service – all that He wants from you is your willingness. He will do the rest.

Father God, here I am, reporting for duty. I do not have a lot, but I give to You what I have. Amen.

THE SACRIFICE OF YOUR FAITH

But even if I am being poured out like a drink offering on the sacrifice and service coming from your faith, I am glad and rejoice with all of you.

PHILIPPIANS 2:17

In Old Testament times the priests brought animal sacrifices to God so that He would forgive His people. The animal had to be slaughtered and its blood had to flow, then God would accept the sacrifice.

Jesus' blood flowed for you when He died on the cross. Your walk of faith will not always be a picnic. It sometimes requires sacrifices from you. And the sacrifices of your faith are seen in a life committed to serving God.

Father, I am committed to serving You. I know that I may face some difficulties, but to You I will remain faithful. Amen.

YOUR SALVATION

I am not ashamed of the gospel, because it is the power of God for the salvation of everyone who believes: first for the Jew, then for the Gentile.

ROMANS 1:16

Paul was never embarrassed to share the good news about Jesus with other people. It was important to him that every person should hear the message of salvation. He realized that the power of God is in the gospel message which gives salvation to anyone who believes in Him.

Believing in Jesus is still the key that unlocks the door to your salvation. And faith means that you do not need to contribute anything to your redemption. All you need to do is accept the free gift of grace God offers to you.

Thank You, Lord, for Your free gift of grace. Because of You and my faith in You, I am redeemed. Amen.

JESUS WAS A
PERSON LIKE YOU

*For we do not have a high priest who is unable
to sympathize with our weaknesses, but we have
one who has been tempted in every way, just
as we are – yet was without sin.*

HEBREWS 4:15

When God sent His Son into the world, He was both truly God and truly human. Jesus was completely without sin, yet He was also tempted just as we are. But He never succumbed to temptation.

Because Jesus was a person just like us, He knows exactly what we are going through when we face temptations. He can sympathize with your human weaknesses. And He promises to help you and to strengthen you when temptations come your way.

Lord, when I am tempted, I look to You for help and strength.
Amen.

July 27

PURE THOUGHTS

*Finally, brothers, whatever is true, whatever is noble,
whatever is right, whatever is pure, whatever is lovely,
whatever is admirable – if anything is excellent
or praiseworthy – think about such things.*

PHILIPPIANS 4:8

*P*aul says that the Philippians should make sure that their thoughts reflect the things that are important to God. Their thoughts should focus on everything that is good and perfect rather than wasting time thinking about sinful and worthless things.

The things that you think about determine how you look at life. That is why you should make an effort to keep your thoughts pure. Think only of those things that are beautiful and worthwhile and your life will reflect the positive thoughts that you think.

Father God, help me to keep my thoughts focused on the things of heaven, rather than the things of this earth.

Amen.

GOD IS ALWAYS RIGHT

You have made known to me the path of life;
you will fill me with joy in your presence,
with eternal pleasures at your right hand.

PSALM 16:11

$\mathcal{T}$he psalmist knows the truth that the secret of true joy is found only in God, and that He always gives the very best to His children. Even so, we still go through hard times in our lives. In these times we can depend on God's support.

During the difficult times, we simply need to hold God's hand tighter. What He does is always right. What He brings into your life is always good. What He has planned for your life is always the best for you.

Father, I have reached the end of my tether. I cling to You in faith, knowing that You will be with me and will help me.

$\mathcal{A}men.$

CONTROL YOUR THOUGHTS

We take captive every thought
to make it obedient to Christ.

2 CORINTHIANS 10:5

*T*he secret to controlling negative thoughts is to ask yourself if God would be pleased with the things that you are thinking. Ask Him to purify your thoughts and help you to reject all negative and wrong thoughts.

The next time you begin to think negative thoughts, thoughts that are not appropriate for a Christian, you need to consciously take those thoughts captive. You can control your thoughts with God's help, and be obedient to God.

Lord, purify my thoughts and remove any negative, wrong thoughts from my mind. Amen.

JOY IN HARD TIMES

Though the fig tree does not bud and there are no grapes on the vines ... yet will I rejoice in the LORD, I will be joyful in God my Savior.

HABAKKUK 3:17-18

Christians have a unique characteristic – they can praise God even when they are in the middle of trials and tribulations because they know that He is fully in control.

Habakkuk could continue to rejoice in spite of the fact that everything was going wrong in his life. When you have absolute trust in God, you too will be able to keep rejoicing – even though you might not understand why God sometimes allows such difficult things in your life to happen.

Lord, I do not always understand why I have to go through certain things, but I trust that You are in control and have only what is best planned for me. Amen.

July 31

GOD'S GUIDELINES

Do not be overcome by evil,
but overcome evil with good.

ROMANS 12:21

*C*hildren of God should not allow the negative things in their lives to get the upper hand. They should put on the armor of God and resist the devil every day. They should take care to do the things that God asks of them.

This can only be achieved if you know your Bible well. The guidelines that God lays down in His Word should clearly be seen in your life.

Father, I put on Your armor, devoting my time to daily devotions, Bible study and prayer. Amen.

August

SEE THE IMAGE OF GOD IN PEOPLE

So God created man in his own image, in the image of God he created him; male and female he created them.

GENESIS 1:27

It is amazing that God, who is so holy and almighty, created people in His image and with His characteristics in them, and that He appointed us to be His ambassadors on earth.

Because you were created in God's image, you should also strive to see the image of God in others you meet, no matter how sinful or unworthy they may seem. You should live each day in such a way that you represent your Lord in a worthy manner.

Lord, help me to live in such a way that others can see You in me. Amen.

SINCERE HUMILITY

But by the grace of God I am what I am,
and his grace to me was not without effect.

1 CORINTHIANS 15:10

*T*alented people run the risk of becoming so chuffed with themselves and their achievements that they lose sight of who gave them their gifts in the first place.

None of us has anything that we did not receive from God. Therefore we have no reason or right to become puffed up about anything.

Sincere humility means that you give God the glory and honor for each one of your achievements. You are what you are by the grace of God.

Father, everything I have and everything I've achieved is from You. I am who I am because of Your grace and nothing else.

Amen.

CHILDREN OF GOD

*I have been crucified with Christ and
I no longer live, but Christ lives in me.*

GALATIANS 2:20

In the letter to the Galatians, Paul writes that he has been crucified with Christ and now lives for God. His old, sinful self belongs in the past, and he no longer lives. It is Christ who lives in him.

Children of God need to be prepared to write their own obituary so that God can live in them. To be made holy means that you decrease, and God increases.

Lord God, the past me no longer exists, because You made me into a new person. Now I live for You. Amen.

YOUR OWN THOUGHTS

*As water reflects a face, so a
man's heart reflects the man.*

PROVERBS 27:19

*J*ust as you look in a mirror to get an idea of what you look like, you discover exactly who you are when you analyze your thoughts. The things that you think are reflected in the way you live your life.

If you think negative thoughts, you will be a negative person. If you discipline yourself to think positive thoughts, your life will reflect a positive approach.

You are what you think. What do you see in the mirror of your own thoughts?

Purify my thoughts, Lord. I don't want to think anything other than that which is godly and positive, and pleasing in Your sight. Amen.

YOU KNOW A PERSON BY HIS WORDS

"The good man brings good things out of the good stored up in his heart, and the evil man brings evil things out of the evil stored up in his heart. For out of the overflow of his heart his mouth speaks."

LUKE 6:45

Out of the fullness of your heart, your mouth speaks. The things that reside in your heart and mind come out in the things that you say and in the way that you live.

Out of the innermost parts of good people, good things come forth. But bad things will eventually come out of bad people. If you listen carefully to what people say, you will understand what their hearts look like.

A tree is known by its fruit, and people by their words.

Father, when people hear me speak or see the way I live, let them see only what is good and pleasing to You. Amen.

A MIRROR OF GOD'S GLORY

*And we, who with unveiled faces all reflect
the Lord's glory, are being transformed into his
likeness with ever-increasing glory, which
comes from the Lord, who is the Spirit.*

2 CORINTHIANS 3:18

All people are born sinful. But when they are born again, their lives change completely. They become mirrors in which others can see how great and glorious the God whom we worship is.

Each Christian should reflect the glory of God. When people look at you they should be aware of God's glory. And the longer you know Him the more you should be changed into the image of Jesus.

Lord God, let the way I live be a perfect reflection of a child of God. Let my life sing Your praise and bring You glory.

Amen.

August 7

YOU BELONG TO GOD

There is no fear in love. But perfect love drives
out fear, because fear has to do with punishment.
The one who fears is not made perfect in love.

1 JOHN 4:18

*T*rue love has a way of dissipating fear, as mist dissolves in the sun. Those who truly love no longer fear punishment. If there are still numerous fears in your life, it means only one thing: you are not yet completely saturated by the love of God.

Ask God to give you more of His love without measure. Because you belong to God, His perfect love will cause every fear in your life to subside.

Thank You, Father, for giving me Your love without measure.
Because You love me, I need not fear anything. Amen.

GOD IS NOT SATISFIED WITH SECOND BEST

"Yet I hold this against you:
You have forsaken your first love."

REVELATION 2:4

*I*n many marriages, the passion of honeymoon love disappears after a while, and the same happens to many of us in our relationship with God.

One day we wake up to find the bubbling joy that we experienced when we were born again has disappeared, and we don't love God with the fiery passion we had at first.

God is never satisfied with second best. He wants your love for Him to increase in fervor. He wants it to always be a "honeymoon" love.

Heavenly Father, let me never lose my love for You. Let my love for You increase every day. Amen.

August 9

OBEDIENCE TO
GOD'S LAW

*But if anyone obeys his word, God's love is truly made
complete in him. This is how we know we are in him.*

1 JOHN 2:5

The love of God blossoms in those people who are obedient to the things that He asks of us in His Word. In such people, the love of God achieves its full purpose.

Through our obedience to God's law and commandments we show other people that we live close to Him.

Your love for God and your obedience to His law can't be separated from each other. The one is the natural result of the other.

*Father, love for You means obedience to Your Word. Help me
to show my love for You through my obedience to Your Word.*

Amen.

ALL-SUFFICIENT GRACE

"My grace is sufficient for you, for my power is made perfect in weakness."

2 CORINTHIANS 12:9

*P*aul begged God to remove the thorn in his flesh, but God did not answer his prayer in the way that he wanted it answered.

God told him that His grace is sufficient for him, that His strength comes to its fullest power when our strength comes to an end.

God offers you His all-sufficient grace, especially when you are at your weakest. When you have no strength, He puts His godly strength at your disposal.

Lord, when I have no strength left, You graciously give me Yours. Thank You. Amen.

ADVERSITY

Rejoice in the Lord always. I will say it again: Rejoice!

PHILIPPIANS 4:4

The letter to the Philippians encourages us to be joyful. But this joy is specifically described: we should rejoice at all times – even when things happen that are not to our liking. When we go through trials and tribulations they bring us closer to God.

To rejoice when we face adversity is difficult but it is exactly in such times that others can see that you belong to God.

Father, when times are difficult, it seems impossible to rejoice in my circumstances. But I can rejoice in You, because You are with me. Amen.

August 12

SHARE YOUR FAITH

Consequently, faith comes from hearing the message,
and the message is heard through the word of Christ.

ROMANS 10:17

God needs witnesses in His Kingdom – people who will make the sharing of the gospel of Jesus Christ their life's purpose; people who will carry the good news of the salvation of Christ to those who have never heard it. No one can believe unless they have heard the gospel message.

If you believe in God, you have a responsibility not only to live out your faith, but also to share it with people around you.

Father, help me to be a witness for You, to share the good news of Your salvation with others. Amen.

THE LIGHT OF GOD

You, O LORD, keep my lamp burning;
my God turns my darkness into light.

PSALM 18:28

*T*he children of God can do anything when they know that God is with them. The God whom we worship makes their lamps burn brightly. His presence brings light into their lives when everything around them is dark.

If you believe in God you can courageously face all the challenges that come your way. You will not shirk from any situation, because God is your helper. He will always turn your darkness into light.

In the darkest moments of my life, Your presence, Lord, is the strong light that guides me through. *Amen.*

August 14

A HEAVY BURDEN

"Come to me, all you who are weary and burdened, and I will give you rest. ... For my yoke is easy and my burden is light."

MATTHEW 11:28, 30

*J*esus came to offer weary, overburdened people His rest. He invites them to put the heavy burden of their problems on His shoulders, and promises that He will give a lighter yoke in exchange.

Most of us are bone weary from carrying the burden of tomorrow's what-ifs together with the guilt of yesterday. God offers to carry your burden for you and to give you rest. Don't put off replying to His invitation.

Heavenly Father, I lay my guilt over yesterday and my worries of tomorrow at your feet. Please take control of my yesterdays and tomorrows so that I can rest in Your peace. Amen.

LESSONS OF LIFE

In this you greatly rejoice, though now for a little while you may have had to suffer grief in all kinds of trials. These have come so that your faith – of greater worth than gold, which perishes even though refined by fire – may be proved genuine.

1 PETER 1:6-7

We all experience problems from time to time. When things in our lives test our faith, we should realize that it is actually a good thing. Just as gold is purified through fire, problems purify our lives because they test the genuineness of our faith.

That is why we should rejoice when we face trials. God uses difficulties to test us at times – He wants to see if we have learned the lessons He has taught us well enough to pass them on to others.

Father, I know that times of testing are necessary in order for our faith to grow, but that doesn't mean that they are easy. Help me to stay steadfast in my faith during such times.

Amen.

WITHSTAND TEMPTATION

*No temptation has seized you except what is
common to man. And God is faithful; he will not
let you be tempted beyond what you can bear.
But when you are tempted, he will also provide
a way out so that you can stand up under it.*

1 CORINTHIANS 10:13

God promises that He will not allow any temptation to come our way that we will not be able to handle. He promises that when temptations come our way, He will give us the strength to make the right decisions and the strength to carry through on the decisions we make.

God does not always remove the temptations in your life, but He gives you a way of escape. He shows you how you can resist those temptations.

Lord, thank You for showing me a way out when I come face to face with temptation. You give me the strength I need to resist it. Amen.

THROUGH ALL ETERNITY

*Will the Lord reject forever? Will he never show his
favor again? Has his unfailing love vanished forever?
Has his promise failed for all time? Has God forgotten to
be merciful? Has he in anger withheld his compassion?*

PSALM 77:7-9

The psalmist is heartbroken because he feels that God
has abandoned him. He feels that he will never again
stand within the light of God's mercy. He cannot understand why God seems to be acting so differently from the
ways He acted in the past.

If you call out to God and it seems that He does not
answer you, you might be inclined to think that He has
changed. But that cannot happen: God is the same yesterday, today and forever.

*Father, no matter what happens, You never change. You will
always be there, always ready to help Your children.*

Amen.

THE PROBLEMS OF TODAY

Because he himself suffered when he was tempted,
he is able to help those who are being tempted.

HEBREWS 2:18

*M*any Christians become very discouraged when crises erupt in their lives. They feel as though they cannot take one more step. But it is not necessary for them to feel this way. God is ready to carry His children when times are hard. He is there to help, but He does so one day at a time.

You do not need to try to solve all the problems of yesterday and tomorrow along with all the troubles of today. Live one day at a time and you will find that you are able to handle every situation with God's help.

Father, when I feel overwhelmed in the midst of crises and like I can no longer walk, You will be there to carry me.

Amen.

DISAPPOINTMENTS

Shall we accept good from God, and not trouble?

JOB 2:10

Even though Job experienced unbelievable hardship and pain, he still believed in God.

If we accept the good things that God sends our way, then it is only logical that we should accept the bad things that come our way too. Every person who has ever lived goes through good and bad times. Learn to accept both from God.

We are all disappointed by bad things that happen in our lives but we can learn from these disappointments. Your disappointments are often God's appointments.

Lord, thank You for being with me through challenging times. Please open my eyes so that I may learn from them.

Amen.

OPPORTUNITIES FOR WORSHIP

*But I will sing of your strength, in the morning
I will sing of your love; for you are my fortress,
my refuge in times of trouble.*

PSALM 59:16

David wrote this psalm when he was fleeing from the soldiers Saul had sent to kill him. His situation left much to be desired.

He prayed for God's protection and still found reasons to praise God in the midst of his danger. He was able to turn his crisis into an opportunity to worship God.

When you turn your problems into opportunities for worship, God will intervene in your situation and you will be able to carry on with a song of praise.

Father, help me to be like David and turn my crises into opportunities to worship You. Amen.

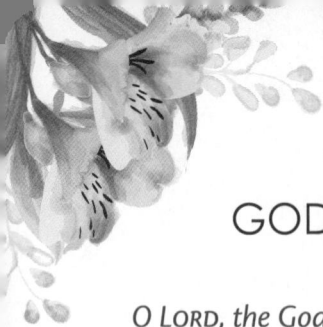

GOD IS WITH YOU

*O LORD, the God who saves me, day and night
I cry out before you. May my prayer come
before you; turn your ear to my cry.*

PSALM 88:1-2

Psalm 88 is another psalm in which the writer faced great distress. Each day he asked God to help him because his strength was gone. Things were going so badly for him that he was not far from death's door. He begged God to change his circumstances.

When you go through hard times, you can unreservedly seek help from God. The Bible assures us that God is with us during hard times. He is always prepared to help us when we ask Him.

Lord, thank You for being there when I need You most. Thank You that I can call on You during difficult times and know that You will answer. Amen.

TRUST THE LORD

I wait for the LORD, my soul waits,
and in his word I put my hope.

PSALM 130:5

*T*he psalmist reconfirms his trust in the Lord when he faces severe difficulties. He realizes that God loves His children and forgives them again and again.

When the Lord allows troubles to come your way and they prevent you from serving Him wholeheartedly, He wants you to trust Him for a solution rather than just complain about it.

Heavenly Father, I find myself in trouble again. Please help me. Please forgive me for constantly complaining instead of trusting You. Amen.

GOD IS ALWAYS
THERE FOR YOU

I have set the Lord always before me.
Because he is at my right hand, I will not be shaken.

PSALM 16:8

*C*hildren of the Lord are assured that they are never alone. God is with them even when things do not go well. Because He is in their lives He ensures that they will not stumble and He keeps them safe.

When you go through difficult times, you can also be assured that God is with you. How you work through your difficulties is up to you, but the mere fact that God is always with you makes it easier from the start.

Lord, I praise You because You are always with me. Even in difficult times I praise You because You have promised to never leave me. Amen.

YOU BELONG TO GOD

*When he heard this, Jesus said, "This sickness
will not end in death. No, it is for God's glory
so that God's Son may be glorified through it."*

JOHN 11:4

$\mathcal{S}$ometimes things happen to God's children that we cannot understand or explain. They fall ill or lose their jobs. They pray but it seems that God does not answer. In such times they cannot understand why God does not intervene to prevent these things from happening. But God often uses pain or suffering to bring glory to His name. He uses them to reveal His strength.

If you keep your joy and faith, and trust God when you face sickness and death, people will see that you have faith in God.

Lord, through every challenge, fear or difficulty I face, I will remain steadfast in prayer and firm in my faith. Amen.

GOD'S COMFORT

When anxiety was great within me,
your consolation brought joy to my soul.

PSALM 94:19

*T*he psalmist testifies that God's comfort makes him calm and peaceful in times of unrest. We all desperately need God's comfort and peace in the restless world we live in.

Pray that God will make His comfort available to you and will calm your restlessness. God's comfort can turn your restless, anxious heart into one filled with peace. He will give you an inner peace and serenity that no one will ever be able to take away from you.

Father God, bless me with Your comfort in difficult times. Fill my heart with Your peace and rest when I feel overwhelmed and anxious. Amen.

BRING YOUR ANXIETIES TO GOD

"Therefore I tell you, do not worry about your life ... Is not life more important than food, and the body more important than clothes? ... For the pagans run after all these things, and your heavenly Father knows that you need them."

MATTHEW 6:25, 32

*B*ecause we belong to God we do not need to worry about the future. In the Sermon on the Mount, Jesus promised us that God, who cares for the flowers and the birds, will do the same for His children.

God promises to care for you too. So you need no longer be anxious about anything. Worry gets you nowhere. Rather bring your worries to God. You will find that they will dissipate like mist before the sun.

Heavenly Father, You are my provider. You know exactly what I need and I rest assured that I will never be in want because You watch over me. Amen.

TIME IS PRECIOUS

*Be very careful, then, how you live – not as
unwise but as wise, making the most of
every opportunity, because the days are evil.*

EPHESIANS 5:15-16

*E*ach person has the same amount of time at their disposal– twenty-four hours a day. And yet there are many people who achieve nothing with the time allotted to them while others move mountains in the same amount of time.

What do you do with the time that God has given you? Time is precious, use it effectively: you can choose to waste your time or use it profitably. You have exactly enough time each day to do just what needs to be done. Ensure that you put your time to the best use each day.

Lord, help me to make the most of my time, using it wisely to serve You. Amen.

STAY QUIET

A man who lacks judgment derides his neighbor,
but a man of understanding holds his tongue.

PROVERBS 11:12

*T*he things that we say about other people can have a big impact on their lives. And what we say about others says a lot about who we are.

Someone who speaks derisively of others has little compassion. Someone who understands people will remain silent rather than drawing attention to negative aspects of a person's character.

Do you enjoy gossiping about other people? If you have nothing positive to say about others, it is best to rather keep quiet.

Father, help me to hold my tongue, to not gossip or say bad things about others. May the only words that leave my mouth be pleasing in Your sight. Amen.

PRAISE GOD

*When I consider your heavens, the work of
your fingers, the moon and the stars, which you
have set in place, what is man that you are mindful
of him, the son of man that you care for him?*

PSALM 8:3-4

As the psalmist gazes at the wonder of God's creation, he cannot help but be impressed by the greatness and power of God. At the same time he realizes how small and insignificant he is. He is overwhelmed when he considers that God actually thinks about each person and cares for us.

You should take time to note the beauty of nature each day, and grow in awareness of the greatness and awesomeness of God. And you should praise Him and thank Him for the wonders of His creation.

Creator God, when I think of the mighty hand that created the world and everything in it, I am awestruck. There really is no God like You. Amen.

August 30

OUR FAITH IS STRENGTHENED

Blessed are those who dwell in your house; they are ever praising you. Blessed are those whose strength is in you, who have set their hearts on pilgrimage.

PSALM 84:4-5

People who frequent the house of God find that things go well for them. They do not cease to praise God because they live in His presence and among other believers. These people find their strength in God.

Church attendance and fellowship with other believers is necessary because it strengthens your faith. Ensure that you do not neglect attending church services. Make sure that you feel at home in God's house.

Father, I long to spend more and more time with You. Help me to never neglect spending time with You or my fellow believers. Amen.

GOD IS YOUR SHEPHERD

*The LORD is my shepherd, I shall not be in want.
… Even though I walk through the valley of the
shadow of death, I will fear no evil, for you are with
me; your rod and your staff, they comfort me.*

PSALM 23:1, 4

Shepherds in biblical times had to look after their sheep. They protected the flocks against dangers and ensured that they had sufficient food and water. And when they had to go through dangerous places, the presence of the shepherd guaranteed their safety.

If the Lord is your shepherd, He promises that His goodness and love, His strength and protection will be with you all the days of your life. You can confidently entrust your life into His hands.

Lord my Shepherd, I know that I am safe in Your hands, because You have promised Your children Your strength, love, goodness and protection. Amen.

September

September 1

GOD'S UNCONDITIONAL LOVE

Give thanks to the LORD, for he is good.
His love endures forever.

PSALM 136:1

*V*arious psalms declare the endlessness of God's love. *"His love endures forever"* is not only the introduction to Psalm 136, but it appears 26 times in the psalm itself.

God's unconditional love for us is the foundation of our love for one another, and the Bible assures us that there is no end to His wonderful love. Like the psalmist, we should thank and praise the Lord each day for His eternal love.

Lord, I praise You for Your unfailing love that stretches far beyond my understanding. Amen.

THE PROMISES OF JESUS

*Then Jesus told him, "Because you have seen
me, you have believed; blessed are those
who have not seen and yet have believed."*

JOHN 20:29

Thomas would not believe that Jesus had really risen from the dead. He insisted that he would only believe if he saw Jesus with his own eyes. When Jesus did appear to him, he bowed before Him and declared his faith. But Jesus told him that people who believe without seeing are blessed indeed.

Ask God to increase your faith so that you may live by faith, not by sight (see 2 Cor. 5:7). Then, without having to see, you will believe that each one of Jesus' promises is true.

Father God, I do not have to see to believe that You are faithful to keep Your promises. Amen.

KEEP BELIEVING

*Then Jesus answered, "Woman, you have great
faith! Your request is granted." And her
daughter was healed from that very hour.*

MATTHEW 15:28

A Canaanite woman brought her sick child to Jesus so that He could heal her. She refused to just give up when Jesus said He would not. She persisted in asking for help until finally Jesus, because of her faith, healed her child.

Sometimes we ask God for things and we don't seem to get "Yes" for an answer. If you are prepared to keep believing and to keep asking, God will fulfill your desires as long as they are in line with His will.

Father, I know that You do not answer all prayers in the way we want You to. But You know what is best for us. Therefore, let Your will be done in our lives. Amen.

JESUS CAN COMFORT YOU

May our Lord Jesus Christ himself and God our Father, who loved us and by his grace gave us eternal encouragement and good hope, encourage your hearts.

2 THESSALONIANS 2:16-17

Paul, in his letter, tells the Thessalonians that Jesus loves them very much. As proof of this love He comforts the Christians with the good news that they are on their way to a wonderful eternity in heaven.

When you are feeling downhearted, Jesus can comfort you because He was human just as you are. The comfort He gives you is lasting comfort that can never be taken away from you. You too can know that a wonderful future awaits you in heaven.

I rejoice in Your glorious name, Lord. Because of You, I have the wonderful promise of eternal life to look forward to.

Amen.

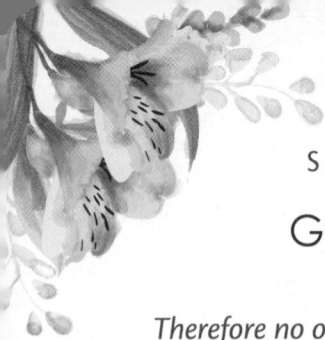

GOD'S LAW

*Therefore no one will be declared righteous
in his sight by observing the law; rather,
through the law we become conscious of sin.*

ROMANS 3:20

People are not set free from their sins because they keep God's law. The only thing the law can do is to show us what is right and wrong; it cannot help us not to commit sins.

God's law is a map that shows God's children how to live. Only the map of God's law can show you how to safely negotiate the land-mined terrain of sinfulness.

Lord, I meditate on Your Word and Your commandments. Let them guide me in every area of my life so that I may live a godly life in service of You. Amen.

TALK LESS

Set a guard over my mouth, O Lᴏʀᴅ;
keep watch over the door of my lips.

PSALM 141:3

*T*he psalmist prays that God will help him not to say the things he shouldn't. He asks that God will help him to choose his words carefully.

James tells us that the person who does not stumble over what he says is perfect; he can then control the rest of his body (see Jas. 3:2).

We each have two ears and only one mouth. It would therefore seem logical that we should talk much less and become much better listeners!

Father, help me to listen more and talk less. Help me to think before I speak and to only speak uplifting words. Amen.

GET OUT OF THE MUD BATH OF SIN

Do you not know that your body is a temple of the Holy Spirit, who is in you, whom you have received from God? You are not your own; you were bought at a price. Therefore honor God with your body.

1 CORINTHIANS 6:19-20

*J*esus paid in full for our sins with His blood on the cross. Now we need to live as people who have been set free. Our bodies are the temple of the Holy Spirit and we should glorify God with our bodies.

If you believe in Jesus, then your body is also a temple. It is impossible for Christians to wallow in the mud bath of sin and to think that they will remain clean. Live in such a way that God will be glorified in your body.

Lord Jesus, because of Your sacrifice, sin no longer has control over me as I now live in Your grace. Please help me to live in such a way that it will bring honor to Your name. Amen.

LIVE OUT YOUR FAITH

*Therefore, my brothers, be all the more eager
to make your calling and election sure. For if
you do these things, you will never fall.*

2 PETER 1:10

$\mathcal{P}$eter tells us that we should grab every opportunity to live for the Lord. Through the things that we do, other people should be able to see that God called us and that we are His children, living according to His will. If we get this right then we will not continue to struggle with sins in our lives.

Does your lifestyle reflect that you belong to God? If you are prepared to live out your faith in hard times, your life will be a reflection of your faith.

*Father, take control of my life and guide me in everything I do
so that my lifestyle might reflect You.* $\mathcal{A}men.$

September 9

GENUINENESS OF FAITH

*In this you greatly rejoice, though now for a little
while you may have had to suffer grief in all kinds
of trials. These have come so that your faith – of
greater worth than gold, which perishes even
though refined by fire – may be proved genuine.*

1 PETER 1:6-7

Children of God can rejoice when they face hard times
because they know that God uses these situations to
bring about positive results in their lives and to determine the genuineness of their faith.

Just as the purity of gold is tested by fire, God tests
the genuineness of your faith through difficult situations
that come your way while you are on earth. See if you can
manage to rejoice when you face trials and tribulations!

*Father God, I will still rejoice in You even in times of difficulty,
because I know that You will let everything work out for the
best. Amen.*

GOD'S SUPPORT IS ASSURED

*God has surely listened and heard my voice
in prayer. Praise be to God, who has not rejected
my prayer or withheld his love from me!*

PSALM 66:19-20

*T*he psalmist testifies that God hears his prayer and delivers him in his need. He promises that he will tell others in the congregation of how God delivered him and praise God before everyone.

We can always find help and support from God. His support is so certain that you, like the psalmist, can know that your prayer has already been heard even while you are still praying. And don't forget to honor God before others when He helps you!

Lord, even before I think to pray, You already know what I need. Thank You for being my Helper always. *Amen.*

A CELEBRATION OF LIFE

All the days of the oppressed are wretched,
but the cheerful heart has a continual feast.

PROVERBS 15:15

If you tend to get depressed and are worried about all kinds of things, then it is pretty certain that life will not be very pleasant for you. But if you try to be cheerful each day and focus on the positive things in your life, and if you help others to focus on those things too, then your life will be a celebration.

If you make an effort to be joyful and friendly every day, your life will become a celebration and you will make the world a pleasant place for the people around you.

Father, I enter today focused on You and Your blessings. Your abundant blessings and goodness fill me with exuberant joy. Help me to share this joy with everyone I meet. Amen.

September 12

GOD KNOWS EVERYTHING

O LORD, you have searched me and you know me. You know when I sit and when I rise; you perceive my thoughts from afar.

PSALM 139:1-2

*I*t is easy to hide things from people. But God knows everything. He already knows what you are thinking even before you have formulated your thoughts or put them into words. Your whole life is an open book before Him. He sees right through you. He knows all there is to know about you.

You can never hide from God. He knows everything about you. He knows each one of your hidden sins. He even knows what you think. Live so that you need never be ashamed before God.

Father, I am an open book to You. Nothing that I do or say or think is hidden from You. Please help me to live in such a way that I never have to be ashamed of my actions. Amen.

TELL THE LORD YOUR PROBLEMS

My soul is weary with sorrow;
strengthen me according to your word.

PSALM 119:28

David was often worried because of the dozens of things that went wrong in his life. He often had to flee from his enemies and frequently found himself in life-threatening situations. But David knew where he could turn for help. In this psalm, he testifies that God has always helped him.

If there are situations in your life that make you anxious, problems for which you cannot find solutions, tell them to the Lord – He will give you the strength to solve them and perseverance to overcome them.

Lord, I give You all my worries, all my fears. Give me the strength and the wisdom to solve them in accordance with Your will. Amen.

GOD PROTECTS HIS CHILDREN

The Sovereign LORD is my strength; he makes my feet like the feet of a deer, he enables me to go on the heights.

HABAKKUK 3:19

A deer jumps from rock to rock with agility and confidence. And God protects His children and enables them to find a path through their difficulties. He wants to give you the strength you need each day and to protect you when you are in perilous situations.

Next time you face a dangerous situation in your life and it feels as if you are about to lose your footing, cling to God and declare, *"When I said, 'My foot is slipping,' your love, O LORD, supported me"* (Ps. 94:18).

Father God, when times are tough, I need not fear falling, because You will be right there to catch me and to carry me the rest of the way. Amen.

GROW IN HARDSHIPS

Praise be to the God and Father of our Lord Jesus Christ, the Father of compassion and the God of all comfort, who comforts us in all our troubles, so that we can comfort those in any trouble with the comfort we ourselves have received from God.

2 CORINTHIANS 1:3-4

God promises to help His children through every difficult situation they face. But He asks that we would, in turn, do the same for other people. He wants us to help and comfort others when they go through crises.

Difficulties can be beneficial for you. Not only do they teach you that God is always near to comfort you, but also hardships give you insight and sympathy for other people's problems. Maybe you can help them through the hard times.

Father, I know that worry won't add a single day to my life, so I give all my cares and all my worries to You. Help me to learn from the difficult times and to persevere. Amen.

CARING LOVE

*"By this all men will know that you are
my disciples, if you love one another."*

JOHN 13:35

*J*ust as a uniform can show what school or organization a person belongs to, our caring love for each other shows people that we belong to Christ. It is our love for other people that distinguishes us as children of God.

The way that Christians love each other is their distinctive feature. It is the one thing through which other people can see that they are different. Does your love show your friends that you belong to Jesus?

Let my love for others, Lord, set me apart as Your devoted child. Amen.

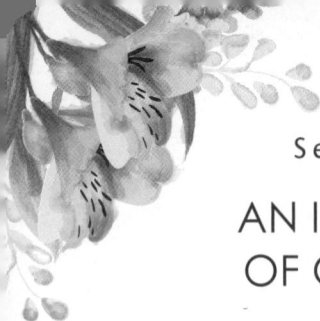

AN ILLUSTRATION OF GOD'S LOVE

*"A new command I give you: Love one another.
As I have loved you, so you must love one another."*

JOHN 13:34

When Jesus was on earth, He exemplified the love of God each day. He was always prepared to help other people. He healed the sick, gave the lame the ability to walk, the deaf the ability to hear and the blind their sight. Jesus really cared for other people, and this was evident in the way He acted.

Just as Jesus was a living illustration of God's love on earth, He wants us to be examples of His love to others.

Father, let me be an example of Your love just like Jesus is an example for me. Amen.

BE THANKFUL ALWAYS

Give thanks in all circumstances,
for this is God's will for you in Christ Jesus.

1 THESSALONIANS 5:18

To be constantly thankful is a way of life. It means that you no longer take things for granted but you know that everything you have is a gift of God's undeserved grace.

Paul, in his letter to the Thessalonian Christians, wrote that it is not enough simply to be thankful; they should be thankful in every situation.

Through faith you can succeed in being thankful in all circumstances. It is often in these difficult situations that God hones you to be a better witness for Him.

Lord, help me to always be thankful. Even in the midst of difficulty, help me to focus on everything I have to be thankful for. Amen.

GOD'S PERFECT LOVE

Do not be anxious about anything, but in everything, by prayer and petition, with thanksgiving, present your requests to God. And the peace of God, which transcends all understanding, will guard your hearts and your minds in Christ Jesus.

PHILIPPIANS 4:6-7

Children of God have no need to worry about anything. All they need to do is tell God about the things they really want, and at the same time to thank Him because He will give them what they ask for. People who get this right live with the peace of God in their lives.

Praise and thanksgiving go hand-in-hand. Once you discover this, you can give the many fears in your life to God in exchange for His perfect peace.

Heavenly Father, I do not need to toil over the things that worry me, because You hear my prayers. I praise You for being the almighty, ever-present Father in my life. Amen.

OUR BROKEN WORLD

Blessed is he whose help is the God of Jacob,
whose hope is in the LORD his God.

PSALM 146:5

*T*hings always go well for the people who depend on God and who go to Him for help. They know that they can confidently keep trusting in God because, in spite of the fact that they live in a broken world, He is preparing a new world for their future.

Our broken world fits into God's Master Plan. Because He is always in control, you can always put your hope in Him. You have Jesus' promise that He has gone to prepare a place for you in heaven.

This world might be broken, Lord, but I can still rejoice and rest in hope, because You have already prepared a place for me in heaven. Amen.

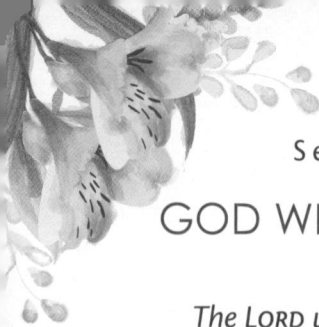

GOD WILL SUPPORT YOU

*The LORD upholds all those who fall
and lifts up all who are bowed down.*

PSALM 145:14

*T*he psalmist knows that God is always there for people who are tired and discouraged. He supports those who are oppressed.

That is why even though many of the psalms begin on a negative note, by the end of the psalm the writers are much more positive. Things are not necessarily better for them but they have faith that God will support them as He has done in the past.

When you feel depressed and discouraged, God promises that He will hold you up and support you. Trust Him to do so!

Father God, in my darkest hours, when I feel most upset and alone, You come to pick me up out of the mud. You love me and that's all that matters. Amen.

GOD KNOWS
YOU PERSONALLY

What is man that you are mindful of him,
the son of man that you care for him?

PSALM 8:4

God is great and almighty while people are insignificant and transitory. There are millions and millions of people in the world, and yet God knows each one of His children. He knows us personally.

God who is so great and almighty knows you personally, too. He knows your name, He thinks about you, He came to offer His love to you – the Bible assures us of all this. And anyone who touches you, touches the apple of His eye!

Father, even though You are Lord over all the earth, You care so much about me that You have even counted the hairs on my head. Thank You for Your incredible love and care for me.

Amen.

September 23

TRUST IN THE LORD

*When I called, you answered me; you made
me bold and stouthearted. The LORD will
fulfill his purpose for me; your love,
O LORD, endures forever – do not
abandon the works of your hands.*

PSALM 138:3, 8

*T*he children of God never call on Him in vain. He always stands ready to help them succeed and He is always prepared to offer His miracle working power to them. That is why, in the long run, things always turn out well for those who trust in Him.

If you trust in the Lord you will be capable of doing great things because He promises you His help, support and strength.

Heavenly Father, I trust in You. My past, my present, my future is in Your hands. With Your strength, I can handle anything that comes my way. Amen.

THE LOVE OF GOD

*This is how we know who the children of God
are and who the children of the devil are: Anyone
who does not do what is right is not a child of God;
nor is anyone who does not love his brother.*

1 JOHN 3:10

*T*here are different ways that our love for the Lord can
be proven: those people who do not do what is right, or
those who do not love others are definitely not children
of the Lord.

By loving all those around you with the love of God,
you make Him visible to the world. This is the guarantee
that you belong to Him. Ask God to give you an abundance
of His love so that it will overflow and touch all
those people you come into contact with.

*Heavenly Father, let my heart overflow with Your blessing of
love, so that I may touch the hearts of others and that they
can see Your love in me. Amen.*

ON THE RIGHT ROAD

Whoever loves his brother lives in the light,
and there is nothing in him to make him stumble.

1 JOHN 2:10

It is possible to differentiate between people who live in the light of God's presence and those who wander around in the darkness of sin. Just look at the way they treat other people.

Those who love others live in the light and God Himself will show them the right road through life. Those who do not love others remain in darkness.

If you love others with the love with which God loves you, this love will keep you on the right road and keep you from stumbling.

Lord God, let Your light shine through me in the way I treat those around me. Help me to love them with the same love that You hold in Your heart for me. Amen.

LITTLE FAITH

But when he asks, he must believe and not doubt,
because he who doubts is like a wave of the sea,
blown and tossed by the wind. That man should
not think he will receive anything from the Lord.

JAMES 1:6-7

*W*hen you pray but do not receive what you pray for,
you should carefully consider whether your unanswered
prayers are perhaps the result of your lack of faith.

Do you really believe that God can – and will – give
you what you ask for? If you still doubt, you should not
expect to receive anything from the Lord.

The reason that you have so many unanswered prayers
is because you have such little faith. People who doubt
do not receive much of what they ask God for in prayer.

Father, remove any doubt from my mind and help me to re-
main steadfast in my faith. Amen.

A CHILD OF GOD

*If anyone considers himself religious and yet
does not keep a tight rein on his tongue, he
deceives himself and his religion is worthless.*

JAMES 1:26

*M*any people say that they are Christians but if you listen to their conversations, you find it hard to believe! They gossip about others, pass on all kinds of untruths and half-truths, and sometimes use swear words and even use the Lord's name in vain. James warns that people who think that they are spiritual but who cannot control their tongues, deceive themselves.

Be warned! If you are a child of God your conversation should show it, otherwise your religion is worthless.

*Father, let every aspect of my life reflect my devotion to You.
Put a guard over my mouth so that I will not gossip or say
anything that is not both true and uplifting. Amen.*

DEPEND ON GOD

*But even if I am being poured out like a drink offering
on the sacrifice and service coming from your faith,
I am glad and rejoice with all of you.*

PHILIPPIANS 2:17

*T*he faith of the Philippians is a sacrifice in the service of God, says Paul. Even if his blood should be poured out as an offering to the Lord, he would still rejoice. His death would help the Philippians to serve God even better.

Faith is not always easy because it requires you to recognize your own limitations and to confess your dependence on God. Only when you realize that you can do nothing on your own, will you develop the kind of faith that God longs for His children to have.

Heavenly Father, help me to develop a strong, immovable faith in You. Amen.

IN DIFFICULT SITUATIONS

When I said, "My foot is slipping,"
your love, O LORD, supported me.

PSALM 94:18

*T*hings happen to each one of us that threaten to knock us off our feet of faith. Then we even begin to question God's love for us. When circumstances threaten to knock you off your feet, God puts His faithful love at your disposal. Hold fast to that and you will remain standing.

You can lean on God when you go through hard times. His faithful love is always there to support you when you cannot stand on your own.

When life tries to knock me down, Lord, I will lean on You. I will trust in Your love for me. Amen.

KEEP YOUR PROMISES

When you make a vow to God,
do not delay in fulfilling it. He has no
pleasure in fools; fulfill your vow.
It is better not to vow than to
make a vow and not fulfill it.

ECCLESIASTES 5:4-5

We tend to make vows and promises to God very glibly when we are in tight spots. But when things begin to get better we often forget the promises we made. The preacher in Ecclesiastes says that we should not let this happen. What we promise to do must be followed through. If you do not think you can keep your promises, you should rather not make any. Keep every promise you make – to people as well as to God.

Father, help me to keep the promises I make. Amen.

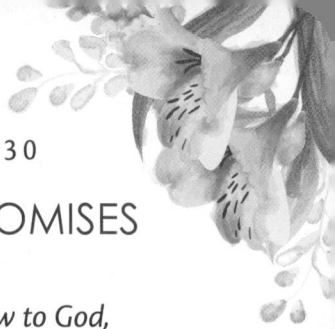

October

EVERYTHING COMES FROM GOD

For who makes you different from anyone else?
What do you have that you did not receive?

1 CORINTHIANS 4:7

We are all innately selfish. Secretly we like to think that we're just a little better than the next person. In our eyes there is no one quite as important as us! This is particularly true if we have been successful and other people look up to us.

But the truth is that not one of us has anything that we did not receive from God. It is easy to become conceited when we do very well. But remember that you have nothing that did not come from God.

Lord, I never want to become so proud that I look down on those around me. Help me to stay humble and to see others as more important than myself. Amen.

GOD'S LOVE IS UNCONDITIONAL

You are my God, and I will give you thanks;
you are my God, and I will exalt you. Give thanks
to the LORD, for he is good; his love endures forever.

PSALM 118:28-29

The Bible has much to say about the extent of God's love. "The earth is full of his unfailing love ... Your love, O Lord, reaches to the heavens, your faithfulness to the skies," writes the psalmist (Ps. 33:5; 36:5). And above all, His love is unconditional.

God's love for you is unending and unrestricted. It does not depend on your good points. It continues forever – in spite of your faults and weaknesses.

Thank You, King of kings, for loving me in spite of my faults and weaknesses. Amen.

GOD IS YOUR FATHER

*For you did not receive a spirit that makes you
a slave again to fear, but you received the Spirit
of sonship. And by him we cry, "Abba, Father."*

ROMANS 8:15

The word *Abba* is the intimate term a child would use when they talk to their dad. It is only through the Holy Spirit that we are able to call the great Creator *Dad*. He makes us children of God and ensures that an unbreakable bond forms between the Father and us.

The presence of the Holy Spirit in your life is your personal spiritual birth certificate; proof that you are God's daughter. Because He lives in you, you can now call God your Father.

With all my heart I give You thanks, Lord God. Because of Your Spirit who lives in me, I can call You my Father and know that You've accepted me as Your child. Amen.

October 4

GOD SHOWS HIS LOVE

May our Lord Jesus Christ himself and God our Father,
who loved us and by his grace gave us eternal
encouragement and good hope, encourage your hearts.

2 THESSALONIANS 2:16-17

If we ever doubt the extent of God's love for us, we simply need to look at Jesus on the cross. God loves us so much that He sent His only Son to be crucified so that, if we believe in Him, we will live forever (see Jn. 3:16). This is the meaning of grace. It is the indisputable evidence of God's love.

If you persist in the faith God will demonstrate His love, grace, comfort, and hope in your life.

Father, I can know beyond a shadow of a doubt that You
love me unconditionally, because when I was still a sinner,
You sent Your only Son to die so that I might be saved.

Amen.

EXPERIENCE HIS PRESENCE

He makes me lie down in green pastures,
he leads me beside quiet waters.

PSALM 23:2

$\mathcal{P}$salm 23 presents us with a pastoral picture of peace and rest, of green hills and peaceful waters, and of a shepherd who watches over his sheep and who ensures their peace and safety.

God wants to be your Shepherd. In a world of unrest and violence, He wants to create a living space for you where you can be happy and safe, and where you will experience His peace and His presence every day.

Let God renew your strength and guide you on the right path.

Heavenly Father, thank You for being the mighty Shepherd who watches over me and ensures my safety. In You I find peace and rest. Amen.

SHARE IN HIS GLORY

God disciplines us for our good,
that we may share in his holiness.

HEBREWS 12:10

It is never pleasant to be punished, but it is good for us. Children who are chastised, later reap the positive fruits of the punishment that has been issued. Someone who learns his lesson by being punished becomes a person who is obedient to God. Such a person is fully committed to God.

God's discipline is always for your best. He draws you closer to Himself through it. And then you will be able to share in His glory. Do not run from His punishment, but learn the lesson God is trying to teach you.

Father, I realize that You are not punishing me out of spite, but out of love, wanting me to be able to reap the benefits of a fruitful life. Amen.

October 7

PEACE AND PROSPERITY

Submit to God and be at peace with him;
in this way prosperity will come to you.

JOB 22:21

When Job rebelled against God because he could not understand why he was being so unfairly punished, his friend Eliphas encouraged him to allow God to teach him through what he was experiencing.

When your relationship with God is right and you willingly submit yourself to Him, you will live in peace and God will cause you to prosper. It is only when you are prepared to yield completely to God that you will have peace and prosperity in your life, even when some of the biggest tribulations are staring you in the eyes.

Father, I long for Your peace in my life. That's why I surrender to You completely. Give me Your Spirit of peace and make me a new person in You. Amen.

PEOPLE'S PROBLEMS

You will call, and the LORD will answer; you will cry for help, and he will say: "Here am I." … If you spend yourselves in behalf of the hungry and satisfy the needs of the oppressed, then your light will rise in the darkness, and your night will become like the noonday.

ISAIAH 58:9-10

God expects His children to be finely tuned when other people go through hard times and to support them in their trials. If we are prepared to help others, then God promises to help us when we call to Him in our distress. He will always be available to provide for us when we go through hard times.

If you see others in distress and help them, God will hear and answer your prayers and will be with you when you really need Him.

Lord God, help me to realize when others go through difficult times and show me how I can comfort and help them.

Amen.

YOU NEED NEVER BE AFRAID

Then he got up and rebuked the winds and the waves, and it was completely calm.

MATTHEW 8:26

*T*he disciples were surprised when Jesus stilled the storm with only a few words. They could not understand how the wind and the waves obeyed Him.

Not only does God have power over nature, but He also has power in the lives of His children. That is why you can confidently ask Him to help you when storms rise up in your life.

Jesus is able to still every storm in your life. That is why, with Him, you need never again be afraid.

Jesus Christ, whenever a storm begins to brew in my life, I turn to You for help and safety. You will still the storm and give me strength. Amen.

GOD HOLDS YOU CLOSE

The eternal God is your refuge,
and underneath are the everlasting arms.

DEUTERONOMY 33:27

God is a hiding place for His children, a hiding place from all dangers. And He promises that His arms are always beneath His children to hold them up.

When life knocks you off your feet, you can confidently trust in God. He promises to keep you safe. And even more – in such times you can know that God is holding you securely. He is your hiding place and His eternal arms are always beneath you.

You can always cling to God when you need safety and comfort in His presence.

Father God, no matter what happens, You are always ready to catch me, to carry me and to help me. Thank You for the wonderful care You show me. Amen.

October 11

HARD TIMES

"In this world you will have trouble.
But take heart! I have overcome the world."

John 16:33

The journey of a thousand miles begins with a single step, says the well-known proverb. A long journey consists of many single steps. And in the same way it is easier to handle hard times one day at a time, one milestone at a time, one win at a time. But the hard times become even easier to overcome if God is on your side.

God promises to carry you day by day, not year by year or month by month. Trust Him daily to help you in your hard times and learn to live one day at a time.

Father, living a hundred miles an hour only causes more stress and worry. Help me to slow down and focus only on today. Amen.

YOU ARE STRONG IN HIM

"My grace is sufficient for you, for my power is made perfect in weakness."

2 CORINTHIANS 12:9

If we believe that we are strong enough to handle the problems in our lives on our own, we will quickly discover how wrong we are. But if we depend on God's strength then things are very different. As soon as we acknowledge our own lack of strength, God puts His strength at our disposal.

When you are strong enough to identify your weaknesses, God's strength will be fully deployed in your life. When you are weak, then you are strong in Him.

Father, I am too weak to go at this alone. Please help me. Be my strength when I am weak and carry me when I can no longer walk. Amen.

October 13

GOD PROMISES
TO HELP US

"'If you can'?" said Jesus. "Everything is possible for him who believes." Immediately the boy's father exclaimed, "I do believe; help me overcome my unbelief!"

MARK 9:23-24

There was no one who could heal the desperate father's disabled son. That is why they struggled to believe that Jesus could do it. But Jesus told him that everything is possible for those who believe. The father confessed his faith on the grounds of this statement and asked Jesus to help him in the areas where he still struggled to believe.

It is completely possible to believe in God and yet still harbor doubts. In such times of doubt, God promises to help you overcome your unbelief.

Father, I believe in You with all my heart, but even I must confess that there are times when doubts fill my mind. Help me to overcome these doubts. Amen.

DO NOT BE DISCOURAGED

Say to those with fearful hearts, "Be strong, do not fear;
your God will come, he will come with vengeance;
with divine retribution he will come to save you."

ISAIAH 35:4

There is no one who has the same amount of courage day after day. Sometimes our situation is so hopeless that even with the best will in the world we cannot seem to keep hoping in God.

Does it feel as though you are near breaking point today? If you know God, you need never be discouraged. He can deliver you out of every difficulty and can give you new strength and courage each day. Therefore, be strong, do not be afraid. Your God is here!

In You, Lord, I find the strength and the courage I need for every day. Amen.

October 15

PRAY ABOUT
YOUR CONCERNS

Do not be anxious about anything, but in everything, by prayer and petition, with thanksgiving, present your requests to God. And the peace of God, which transcends all understanding, will guard your hearts and your minds in Christ Jesus.

PHILIPPIANS 4:6-7

*O*ften we find ourselves anxiously kneeling beside our beds to talk to God. But when we trust Him with our desires and anxieties, He gives us peace in our hearts and minds. Then we leave the place of prayer filled with peace.

When we face severe challenges, God offers us His peace that passes all understanding. If you would like to experience God's peace, you must learn to pray about all your concerns.

Lord, I trust You with my desires and anxieties, laying all my concerns at Your feet in prayer. Thank You for Your incredible peace. Amen.

October 16

THE PEACE OF GOD

*"Peace I leave with you; my peace I give you.
I do not give to you as the world gives. Do not
let your hearts be troubled and do not be afraid."*

JOHN 14:27

When Jesus bade farewell to His disciples, He told them that He was going to His Father. And at the same time He promised that He would leave His peace with them. The peace that He gives is different from the peace the world gives. People who have the peace of Jesus in their lives have no need to worry or fear.

Not only does Jesus bring you peace with God, but also the peace of God. You can make His peace part of your life today.

Lord Jesus, thank You for the peace and grace You offer us. Because of You, we need not fear or worry or ever feel alone.

Amen.

KEEP HOPING

*Against all hope, Abraham in hope believed and
so became the father of many nations, just as it
had been said to him, "So shall your offspring be."*

ROMANS 4:18

Abraham knew that it was no longer possible for God's promise of descendants through him to be fulfilled. Neither he nor his wife could have children. But still he refused to give up hope. He didn't believe those who said it couldn't be done. He believed that God's promise would come to pass, no matter what happened.

If, like Abraham, you can continue to hope, even when it seems that all grounds for hope are lost, then, like him, you will reap the fruit of faith in God's perfect timing.

Heavenly Father, I trust in Your perfect timing for my life. I know You will be faithful to keep Your promises. Amen.

RENEWED RELATIONSHIPS

*Therefore, since we have been justified through faith,
we have peace with God through our Lord Jesus Christ.*

ROMANS 5:1

We see little of the kind of peace the Bible describes in our own lives. All around us we see unrest and violence. But God can still give His children peace. Because we believe in Him, He sets us free to live in peace with Him and with other people.

Peace on earth can best be described as a ceasefire. God's peace refers to renewed relationships: with Him, with ourselves, and with others.

Father, help me to promote peace in my life, in my relationships, in everything I do. *Amen.*

PEACE IN YOUR HEART AND LIFE

I will listen to what God the LORD will say;
he promises peace to his people, his
saints – but let them not return to folly.

PSALM 85:8

The psalmist writes that the Word of God brings peace to His people, to those who faithfully serve Him. If you make God's Word part of your life, then it will bring about peace in your life. Through His Word, you hear Him speak personally to you each day.

Listen carefully to everything that God says to you. If you are obedient to Him, you will experience His peace in your heart and life.

King of kings, I want to obey Your every word. Help me to understand Your will for my life and guide me on a path of obedience to You. Amen.

LASTING PEACE

For he himself is our peace.

EPHESIANS 2:14

Peace is not a state of mind, but a Person, Paul explains to the Ephesians: Christ is our peace. Because Jesus came into the world it became possible for peace to exist between God and mankind, and between people among themselves.

Make sure that you are never without this peace. The peace that Jesus gives is lasting. Because it comes from within, nothing that ever happens to you can take that peace away. All you need to do is have a relationship with Him, and He will give you peace.

Lord Jesus, bless me with Your peace that no one and nothing can take away. Amen.

BE PREPARED TO
BE USED BY GOD

Therefore, my dear friends, ... continue to work out your salvation with fear and trembling, for it is God who works in you to will and to act according to his good purpose.

PHILIPPIANS 2:12-13

It is not all that hard to live as children of God and to do the things He asks us to do. In the long run, God simply wants us to be prepared to be used by Him. If we are willing, He will equip us and help us to do His will.

God will equip you and enable you to do the things that He expects of you. All that you need to do is to be prepared to be used by Him.

Father, I am available, send me. Equip me and help me to do Your will. Amen.

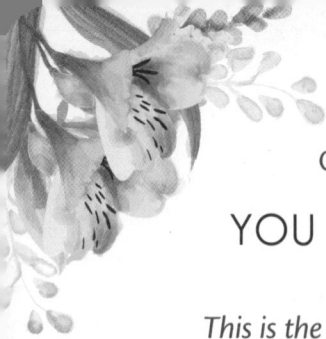

YOU HAVE TODAY

This is the day the LORD has made;
let us rejoice and be glad in it.

PSALM 118:24

*E*ach new day that God gives to His children is a reason to rejoice. It is a day that we can enjoy fully and in which we can do the things we really want to do.

Not one of us knows how many days are left of our lives here on earth. You cannot know how many tomorrows lie ahead of you. But you do have today. Use each moment fully today and enjoy the day. Don't put off for tomorrow what you can do today.

Lord, let me not waste any of the little time I have here on earth. Let me do all I can today, because I don't know how many tomorrows I have left. Amen.

HARD TIMES STRENGTHEN YOUR FAITH

We also rejoice in our sufferings, because we know that suffering produces perseverance; perseverance, character; and character, hope.

ROMANS 5:3-4

Christians can really rejoice when they go through hard times because they have discovered a special secret: hard times form and fashion them so that their faith in God increases. It also helps them to develop a strong Christian character and to believe. Through thick and thin they believe that God's new world waits for them.

Rejoice in your trials and tribulations. Difficulties are always a catalyst that strengthen your faith and give you a brighter hope in God.

Father God, help me to see difficult times as moments in which to strengthen my faith, rather than a time to give up.

Amen.

October 24

SHARE YOUR
HEARTACHE WITH GOD

Hear my prayer, O LORD, listen to my cry for help;
be not deaf to my weeping. For I dwell with you
as an alien, a stranger, as all my fathers were.

PSALM 39:12

The psalmist begs God to listen to his prayer, to hear his cry for help, and not to be unmoved by his tears. He is convinced that the Lord will protect him and that He will care for him in his times of despair.

When sorrow comes your way, the best advice you can follow is to share your pain with God. He is always ready to comfort you, to help you and to care for you.

Lord, You see every tear that rolls over my cheek. You know my deepest hurts. Listen to my prayer for help, comfort me and bring me out of this dark time. Amen.

October 25

THE BEAUTY OF NATURE

Listen to this, Job; stop and consider God's wonders. Do you know how God controls the clouds and makes his lightning flash? Do you know how the clouds hang poised, those wonders of him who is perfect in knowledge?

JOB 37:14-16

God made this world wonderfully well – and He knows all things. When he took Job for a walk through the beauties of His creation, Job realized for the first time how great His wonders are. Finally he knew that God owed him nothing and people have no right to question God.

Don't ever walk blindly through the wonders and beauties of nature, and don't forget to bow in adoration before the Creator of all things.

God, Creator of the Universe, everything in all creation belongs to You. Thank You for Your wonderful creation and constant blessing. Amen.

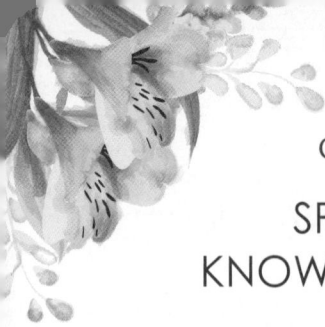

SPREAD THE KNOWLEDGE OF HIM

*For we are to God the aroma of Christ among those
who are being saved and those who are perishing.*

2 CORINTHIANS 2:15

*G*od can do all things, but on earth He chooses to work through His children. He wants us to spread the knowledge of Jesus among the people around us. He uses us wherever we are to make other people aware of Jesus.

God wants your life to be a testimony that rises like incense before Him. He wants to spread the knowledge of Himself through you so that everyone in the world will get to hear His good news first hand.

Lord God, give me the courage and the right words to spread Your good news all over. *Amen.*

REACH OUT

And over all these virtues put on love, which binds them all together in perfect unity. Let the peace of Christ rule in your hearts, since as members of one body you were called to peace. And be thankful.

COLOSSIANS 3:14-15

*T*he most important commandment that God asks of His children is that they love each other. This love is the bond that binds Christians together in perfect unity. And people who love each other in this supernatural way also have God's peace.

When Christians unite and reach out to one another in love it will automatically lead to mutual peace. Make the world a better place with the love of Christ.

Father, I want to share Your love with others. Help me to love those around me with Your unfailing love, even those people I don't really like. Amen.

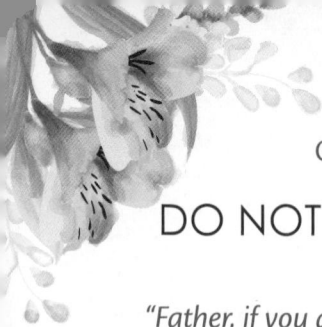

DO NOT PRESCRIBE TO GOD

"Father, if you are willing, take this cup from me; yet not my will, but yours be done."

LUKE 22:42

$\mathcal{S}$ometimes we ask God for things in such a way that we insist on getting our own way. But that's not how prayer works. In Gethsemane, Jesus earnestly prayed that God would remove the cup of suffering from Him, but He was still prepared to subject His will to God's will.

Make very sure that you don't prescribe to God when you come to Him in faith. And don't be disappointed and upset if God answers your prayers differently from how you would have liked the answers to come. Rather, align your will to God's so that your prayer and God's will are one.

Father, I lay my desires, my wants, my needs before You. Please hear my prayer and answer me in accordance to Your will. Let Your will be done here on earth as it is in heaven.

Amen.

THE SECRET OF CONTENTMENT

Enjoy what you have rather than desiring what you don't have.

ECCLESIASTES 6:9

*V*ery few people are satisfied with what they have. We always want more money, a better car, a smarter house and so we forget to be thankful for all those things that God has already given us. What we have is better than what we long for, says the writer of Ecclesiastes.

Therefore, be satisfied with what you have and enjoy what you have. When you discover that the things you already have are better than the things you think you want, you will have found the secret to contentment.

Lord, help me to count my blessings, to appreciate everything I have. But most of all, help me to realize that true contentment and joy does not lie in material possessions, but in You.

Amen.

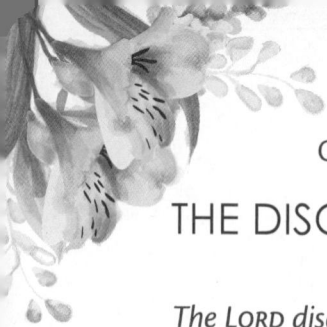

October 30

THE DISCIPLINE OF GOD

The LORD disciplines those he loves, and he punishes everyone he accepts as a son.

HEBREWS 12:6

When the Lord loves someone, He shows them what He expects of them, even though it might sometimes be painful. He acts like parents who truly love their children, and so chastise them because they love them. They want to keep their children on the right road.

No one likes going through painful experiences, but remember that more often than not God's discipline is proof of His love for you – people don't punish children who are not their own!

Heavenly Father, punishment is never easy, but I know that when You punish me it truly is only because You really do love me. Amen.

GOD'S COMFORT

"Blessed are those who mourn,
for they will be comforted."

MATTHEW 5:4

All those who mourn over the pain and hardship of this world are blessed because God Himself will wipe away their tears and comfort them, so Jesus taught in the Sermon on the Mount. The Bible promises us that all our heartache will come to an end when Jesus returns.

Your pain is important to God. He collects every tear you cry and keeps record of them in His book (Ps. 56:8). He is with you throughout your heartaches, comforting you all the time.

Father, even in pain and suffering I can persevere, because I know that one day You will return and wipe away all my tears. On that day, there will be no more pain or suffering – only joy. Amen.

November

GOD OFFERS YOU ETERNITY

For our light and momentary troubles are achieving for us an eternal glory that far outweighs them all.

2 CORINTHIANS 4:17

*O*ur difficulties in this world cannot be compared to the wonderful things that await us in God's new world. And what's more, our times of suffering last for only a short time. God's children will eventually experience a glory that far surpasses our greatest expectations. And it will last forever.

Always remember what the bigger picture is: all earthly problems are merely temporary. Anchor your hope in God who offers you eternal life.

Thank You, Lord, that I do not have to suffer difficulties forever, because I have Your promise of eternal life to cling to.

Amen.

MESSAGE OF HOPE

Always be prepared to give an answer to everyone who asks you to give the reason for the hope that you have.

1 PETER 3:15

When people ask us about the things that God has promised to His children, and which we anticipate so eagerly, we should always be ready to give them an answer and to tell them about our hope. This is the advice Peter gives us.

You too need to be prepared to talk to others about the hope that lives in you. Each Christian carries God's hope – and the responsibility of conveying this message of hope to others rests on you.

Father, prepare me for the day that I will have to give an account to others for the reason for my hope. Help me to say the right thing at the right time and to Your glory. Amen.

GOD HAS ALWAYS BEEN YOUR HELP

The LORD is my strength and my shield; my heart trusts in him, and I am helped. My heart leaps for joy and I will give thanks to him in song.

PSALM 28:7

When the psalmist feels discouraged because things are going so wrong in his life, he reminds himself that God has always helped him in the past. That is why he can believe that God will do so again in the future.

Faith shows the reality of what we hope for; it is the evidence of things we cannot see (Heb. 11:1).

Faith always relies on specific knowledge. You know that God will help you because He has always been your help. Trust Him, and praise Him!

Father God, no matter what happens, I can trust You because You have always been my Rock and my Help. Amen.

YOUR LIFE
WILL CHANGE

*If you confess with your mouth, "Jesus is Lord,"
and believe in your heart that God raised
him from the dead, you will be saved.*

ROMANS 10:9

In his letter to the Romans, Paul explains that it is very easy to be saved. All that you need to do is to confess with your words that Jesus Christ is Lord and believe in your heart that God raised Him from the dead.

Faith and testimony always go hand in hand. And faith and testimony are required of every child of God. If you believe in God and bear witness to Him then your whole life will change.

Lord, I confess with all my heart that I believe in You. I believe that You died for me on the cross, that You were raised from the dead and that You ascended to heaven so that I might be saved and receive eternal life. Amen.

GOD OFFERS YOU HIS MERCY

Yet the LORD longs to be gracious to you; he rises to show you compassion. For the LORD is a God of justice. Blessed are all who wait for him!

ISAIAH 30:18

*T*he prophet Isaiah had a message for the people: God was waiting for an opportunity to show them the extent of His great mercy toward them. He was ready to intervene in their negative circumstances at any moment because of His compassion for them.

And God is waiting to be merciful to you too. He never treats you as you deserve. He offers you His grace and mercy and eagerly waits for you to accept it.

Father, be gracious and merciful to me. Please help me by intervening in my current negative situation. Amen.

HEAVENLY GLORY

Christ in you, the hope of glory.

COLOSSIANS 1:27

*C*hrist lives in each of His children through His Holy Spirit. He made it possible for us to go to heaven one day where we will live with Him forever. He makes it possible for us to hold fast to the hope of the heavenly glory that awaits us.

The Christian's whole life is determined by the fact that we hope in Christ. He earned heavenly glory for each one of His children on the cross.

Jesus died for you, now He lives inside of you. He loves you so much that He would do anything to be with you, or to keep you safe. He is your savior, and the world's.

My entire life, Lord, rests on the fact that You are my Savior. My hope in You is the very reason for my being. I praise You, Lord. Amen.

November 7

RECONCILED WITH GOD

*"Blessed are the peacemakers,
for they will be called sons of God."*

MATTHEW 5:9

$\mathcal{B}$lessed are those people who not only have the peace of God in their lives but who also commit themselves to be peacemakers between people, said Jesus. These peacemakers will be called the children of God.

Before you can become a peacemaker you first need to have the peace of Jesus in your own life, and that is only possible if you have been reconciled to God through Christ. When that happens you will begin to promote peace between people.

Lord Jesus, I long to have Your peace in my life. Fill my heart with Your peace so that I too can be a peacemaker in this world. Amen.

ACKNOWLEDGE YOUR OWN WEAKNESSES

Who is like you, O Lord? You rescue the poor from those too strong for them, the poor and needy from those who rob them. ... Vindicate me in your righteousness, O Lord my God; do not let them gloat over me.

PSALM 35:10, 24

God cares for people who are willing to admit their own weaknesses. He sets them free from enemies that are much stronger than them. The psalmist asks that God will do this for him, and that He will always act fairly toward him.

God will set you free from your enemies. They will not overpower you. But sometimes God first wants you to acknowledge your weaknesses before He will reveal His strength to you, and cause justice to triumph.

Father, open my eyes to my own weaknesses. Help me to acknowledge them and work to better them. Amen.

November 9

DON'T GIVE UP

Praise be to the Lord, to God our Savior,
who daily bears our burdens.

PSALM 68:19

God's children can justly praise Him because He supports them each day. He bears their burdens, and reaches out His hand to help them and guide them.

When you feel as though you cannot go on, don't give up. Try to live each day to the full and trust God for tomorrow. Remember to praise Him every day for His help and faithfulness. Praise Him for His surpassing greatness; praise Him for His great works. Praise Him for renewing your energy. Praise Him for everything.

Almighty Father, I praise You for Your guiding hand in my life. I praise You for Your loving care and blessing. Amen.

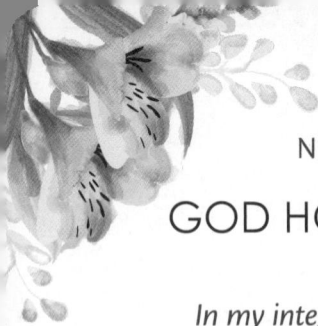

GOD HOLDS YOU TIGHT

*In my integrity you uphold me and
set me in your presence forever.*

PSALM 41:12

A crying baby is soothed very quickly when his mother picks him up and holds him in her arms. In her arms, he feels safe and secure.

The same is true for the children of God. It is reassuring to know that God holds us tight and close to His breast at all times. We are always safe with Him.

God holds His children by the hand. He holds you tight. He is always close to you. He makes sure that you stay near to Him. And in that truth, you can find fullness of peace.

Father, when I feel scared, You hold me close. When I feel alone or in need of comfort, You draw closer. You are the omnipresent Father who promises to never abandon Your children. Amen.

ETERNAL LIFE

*"I give them eternal life, and they shall never perish;
no one can snatch them out of my hand."*

JOHN 10:28

*J*esus told His disciples that He would give eternal life to all those who believe in Him. They will never be lost because no one can pluck them out of His hand. One day they will be with Him in heaven forever.

This promise is meant for you too. If you believe in Jesus, then heaven is yours. He guarantees you eternal life and safety in His hand.

Lord, I look forward to the day when You will come again and take Your children up to heaven. Please help me to be ready for that day. Amen.

PRAY WITHOUT CEASING

"And will not God bring about justice for his chosen ones, who cry out to him day and night? Will he keep putting them off? I tell you, he will see that they get justice, and quickly. However, when the Son of Man comes, will he find faith on the earth?"

LUKE 18:7-8

*J*esus promises that God will listen to His children if they call out to Him day and night. He will not let them wait long for an answer. He will bring them an answer, and quickly at that! All that they need to do is pray.

Sometimes you might get discouraged when you keep on praying and don't receive an answer from God. God promises in His Word that He will help you, and it will be quick. Just keep up your courage for a little while longer!

Father, I will continue to persevere in prayer, because I know that You will answer me when the perfect time comes.

Amen.

IN THE ARMS OF GOD

"As a mother comforts her child, so will I comfort you;
and you will be comforted over Jerusalem."

ISAIAH 66:13

There is only one place where a baby feels completely safe – in his mother's arms. Just as a mother makes her baby feel safe, so God promises to ensure the safety and security of His people.

In the arms of God you will find help and security, stability and safety. With His arms around you, you have nothing to fear. With Him you are safe forever.

So, do not worry, nothing can touch you while you are in God's presence.

Father God, I run to You for safety. Envelop me in Your arms and guide me to where I need to be. Amen.

GOD IS MIGHTY

You are worthy, our Lord and God, to receive glory and honor and power, for you created all things, and by your will they were created and have their being.

REVELATION 4:11

*O*nly God is worthy to receive glory and honor and power because He created all things. This is the testimony of the twenty-four elders when they prostrate themselves before the throne of God in worship.

He alone is the Creator of everything and everyone. It was through His will that the world and all in it came into existence.

God is great, wonderful, almighty, and glorious. He is the Creator of all things. Always remember to praise God, to thank Him and give Him the glory that is due to His name.

Heavenly Father, all glory and power and honor belong to You. You created everything on earth, even the tiniest atom. Therefore we praise You. Amen.

SERENITY

Finally, brothers, whatever is true, whatever is noble, whatever is right, whatever is pure, whatever is lovely, whatever is admirable – if anything is excellent or praiseworthy – think about such things. ... And the God of peace will be with you.

PHILIPPIANS 4:8-9

$\mathcal{S}$tress and anxiety first make their appearance in your thoughts. Therefore, if you can learn to focus your thoughts on the right things then God, who guarantees peace in your life, will give you His peace.

Try to think only restful, relaxing thoughts and suppress the fearful thoughts that try to surface. What you think about will determine whether you become a tense, harried person or whether you will have absolute serenity and inner peace.

Lord God, renew my thoughts. Change them to be only what is pleasing to You. Then Your peace will fill my heart.

Amen.

OBEDIENCE TO GOD

No discipline seems pleasant at the time, but painful.
Later on, however, it produces a harvest of righteousness
and peace for those who have been trained by it.

HEBREWS 12:11

*W*hen a naughty child is disciplined, he realizes that his punishment was for his benefit. Through being punished he learns not to do the things that are wrong.

Later on he discovers that the discipline he received was actually good for him because it taught him to be obedient. "Before I was afflicted I went astray, but now I obey your word" (Ps. 119:67).

Enduring difficulties almost always produces the fruit of peace in your life, because through them you learn to be obedient to God.

Father, guide me along Your path. Help me to obey You and not to complain when You choose to discipline me. I know it is for my own benefit. Amen.

RENEWED DAY BY DAY

*Therefore we do not lose heart. Though
outwardly we are wasting away, yet inwardly
we are being renewed day by day.*

2 CORINTHIANS 4:16

*C*hristians need never be discouraged. Even in the most
difficult times they can persevere because God is always
with them. Each day He renews them from within.

Christians have a light that not even the darkest night
can extinguish. It does not matter how bad things are
on the outside, God renews you day by day within your
heart. And to top it all, you have the assurance that God
will be with you whenever you go through hard times.

*Father, give me the courage to endure hard times. Make me
steadfast in my faith, knowing that You will never leave me.*

Amen.

GOD LISTENS TO YOUR PRAYERS

O people of Zion, who live in Jerusalem, you will weep no more. How gracious he will be when you cry for help! As soon as he hears, he will answer you.

ISAIAH 30:19

Isaiah comforts the grieving people of God. He tells them that they can wipe away their tears. God promises to be merciful to them if they call on Him. He will answer their prayers as soon as He hears them.

This word of comfort is meant for you too. Sometimes it feels as though God is deaf to your pleas when you call out to Him. But that is not possible. He is a merciful God who hears and answers each one of your prayers.

Father, sometimes it feels like You don't hear me when I cry out for help. But I know now that You do. You hear me and You will help me at the right time and in the right way.

Amen.

GOD'S GREATNESS

*God made the earth by his power; he founded
the world by his wisdom and stretched out
the heavens by his understanding.*

JEREMIAH 10:12-13

In this passage, Jeremiah describes the greatness of God. It was God who, through His might, brought the world into existence. When we consider His awesome works in creation, we begin to realize how foolish we are and how little we know.

It is only when you meditate on the greatness of God that you begin to realize your own insignificance and sinfulness. Make time to worship this awesome God.

Father, I praise You for all Your wondrous deeds. No one can fathom all that You've done. Amen.

TRUE LOVE

Dear children, let us not love with words or tongue but with actions and in truth. ... And this is his command: to believe in the name of his Son, Jesus Christ, and to love one another as he commanded us.

1 JOHN 3:18, 23

When Jesus was asked to identify the most important commandment in the Word of God, He did not hesitate to state that it is to love God above all else, and to love others as we love ourselves.

God commands His children to love one another. This is not a debatable issue. And this love needs to be seen in our actions. True love is never just a theory. It is always practical. Your love for the Lord is seen in what you do.

Father, help me to love my neighbor as myself, even the ones who drive me up the wall. Help me to show them Your love through my actions. Amen.

GOD'S LOVE FOR YOU

"For God so loved the world that he gave his
one and only Son, that whoever believes in
him shall not perish but have eternal life."

JOHN 3:16

God loved the world so much that He chose to give His Son so that all those who believe in Him will not be lost but will live forever. God's love is a giving love. It is a love that asks nothing in return.

God's love never asks what it will get from you but always seeks to see what it can give. And this is the kind of love you should foster for other people. Remember the undeserved love Jesus gave you, and pass it on to everyone you meet.

Lord God, You showed me love when I least deserved it. Help me to show that same kind of love to others. Amen.

BROKEN AT THE CROSS

"I tell you the truth, he who believes has everlasting life. I am the bread of life."

JOHN 6:47-48

*J*esus called Himself the bread of life. And He explained that all those who believe in Him already have eternal life. But His body had to be broken on the cross to make eternal life possible for you and me. The cost of turning sinners into children of God was very high.

Faith brings life. Just as we break the bread in communion, Jesus' body was broken for you on the cross so that everyone who believes could receive life.

Lord Jesus, You paid the highest price to save me. Words cannot express how grateful I am. Thank You, Lord. Amen.

FOR YOUR GOOD

*And we know that in all things God works for
the good of those who love him, who have
been called according to his purpose.*

ROMANS 8:28

There is one thing that Christians can be certain of: God has a purpose with everything He allows to happen in their lives. Even the negative things are used to bring about His goal. For those people who love God, those whom He has called to be His children, everything works together for good.

God knows what's best for you. He causes all things to work together for your good if you truly love Him. Don't worry about what the future will bring, have faith in God to be with you very step of the way.

Thank You, Father, for always having my best interest at heart. No matter how bad things may seem, I know that everything will work out for the best because You are in control. Amen.

THE LORD WILL HELP YOU

But I trust in you, O LORD; I say, "You are my God."
My times are in your hands; deliver me from my
enemies and from those who pursue me. ... Be strong
and take heart, all you who hope in the LORD.

PSALM 31:14-15, 24

The psalmist discovered that he could trust God at all times because his whole life was under God's control. That is why he was able to be strong in all circumstances and not give up hope.

Everything that happens to you – even the difficult things – are part of God's plan for your life. If you trust in Him, He will help you. You too can be strong and courageous, even in the midst of a severe crisis.

Father, I don't always understand why I have to go through times of difficulty, but I know that You have a plan for my life and I trust in You. Amen.

GOD GIVES YOU MORE

*Now to him who is able to do immeasurably
more than all we ask or imagine, according to his
power that is at work within us, to him be glory
in the church and in Christ Jesus throughout
all generations, for ever and ever! Amen.*

EPHESIANS 3:20-21

Sometimes the children of God receive very little from Him because they expect so little from Him. God is strong and mighty. His strength is at work in each of His children. He is willing and able to do things for us beyond our wildest dreams, and He gives us far more than we ask of Him.

The God in whom you believe is almighty. He is in a position to give you infinitely more than you ask for. His mercy goes far beyond your prayers and expectations. Always give honor to Him.

Lord God, Your blessings know no boundaries. There is no limit to the goodness that You pour into the lives of Your children every day. Amen.

November 26

NOTHING IS IMPOSSIBLE

*Jesus looked at them and said, "With man
this is impossible, but not with God;
all things are possible with God."*

MARK 10:27

It is not appropriate to judge God by what is humanly possible. Our limitations do not apply to Him. He can make the impossible possible because He is a God of miracles. History shows that God frequently intervenes in the lives of His children in miraculous ways. He is still the same God, and is able to do the same for you today.

God can hear and answer each one of your prayer requests. He has solutions for each of your problems. Nothing is impossible for Him.

Father, even the most impossible situations in my life are not impossible for You. You are more powerful than anything I could ever face. Amen.

IN HIS IMAGE

So God created man in his own image, in the image of God he created him; male and female he created them.

GENESIS 1:27

*W*hen God created people, He created them in His image, with something of His nature in them. People, unlike animals, can distinguish between right and wrong, can love people and can worship God.

There is part of God's nature in you too. Your character and emotions should therefore reflect something of the nature of God. Live in such a way that people who observe you will notice a flicker of God's light in you.

Help me, Lord, to live in such a way that others will be able to see You in me. Amen.

GOD NOTICES YOU

*I pray also that the eyes of your heart may
be enlightened in order that you may know the
hope to which he has called you, the riches of his
glorious inheritance in the saints, and his incomparably
great power for us who believe. That power is like the
working of his mighty strength, which he exerted in
Christ when he raised him from the dead.*

EPHESIANS 1:18-20

We cannot grasp the immensity of God's unlimited might with our human understanding. But the truly remarkable thing is that God not only puts His might, which is stronger than anything else, at our disposal, but also causes that power to work through us.

God is aware of you. He has a special plan for your life. Because you are His child, His illimitable power is at work in your life. You are capable of anything.

Almighty God, Your power is far beyond anything we can hope to understand. It is amazing to think that as Your child, I have access to that power in my life. Amen.

November 29

GIFTS OF GRACE

But to each one of us grace has been
given as Christ apportioned it.

EPHESIANS 4:7

When we begin to compare our average gifts and talents with those of much more gifted friends, we tend to become a little disgruntled and wonder why God passed us over. If this has been the case in your life, have a look at the special abilities that God has entrusted to you.

Even though we have not all been given the same gifts of grace, God has not overlooked even one of us. He has given each one of us a gift that can be used in His service. Use yours to honor Him!

Father, help me to discover all the wonderful abilities You
have gifted me with, so that I can used them to Your glory.

Amen.

HOLD FAST TO
THE PROMISES OF GOD

*Let us hold unswervingly to the hope
we profess, for he who promised is faithful.*

HEBREWS 10:23

God's children can confidently hold fast to every promise of God that is recorded in His Word. God always does what He has promised to do. Hope is a word that focuses on the future. Therefore you can continue to hope in the promises that God will bring to pass in your life. And you can remind Him of these promises.

You can hold onto the promises of God in difficult times because He cannot be unfaithful to His promises.

Father, I cling to every promise You have ever made. I know that You are faithful to keep them. *Amen.*

December

HE DIED ON THE CROSS

Since you are precious and honored in my sight,
and because I love you, I will give men in exchange
for you, and people in exchange for your life.

ISAIAH 43:4

Each person is precious in God's sight. We are so precious that He gives people in our place, nations so that we might live. And He gives even more. He was prepared to give His Son to die on the cross in our place. Jesus gave us His life in exchange for our sins.

You too are precious to God. He knows you by name. He knows all there is to know about you; both good and bad. He loves you so much that He gave His only Son to die for you on the cross.

Heavenly Father, You know everything there is to know about me and yet You still love me. What wonderful news!

Amen.

LIVING FAITH

And without faith it is impossible to please God,
because anyone who comes to him must believe that he
exists and that he rewards those who earnestly seek him.

HEBREWS 11:6

It is impossible to live as God expects us to if we do
not believe in Him. If you really want to stay close to Him
and make His will paramount in your life, it is imperative
to believe that He exists and that He receives with open
arms those people who seek Him.

Faith is the only thing that can bring you into a right
relationship with God. And it is only God who can cause
faith to work in your heart.

Lord, my faith is not based on what the world says, rather it
is based on Your tangible presence and guiding hand in my
life. Amen.

GOD GIVES YOU LIGHT

Who among you fears the LORD and obeys the word of his servant? Let him who walks in the dark, who has no light, trust in the name of the LORD and rely on his God.

ISAIAH 50:10

$\mathcal{D}$ark times come into the lives of every person. In these dark times God wants to be the light in the lives of His children. He wants to offer us His help when we go through crises.

We simply need to take Him at His word, and trust Him. He is always with us when times are hard. And He will cause all things to work together for our good.

God gives you light when you can see no light. He makes things work out well even when things look dark.

Father, I know that even in the most difficult of times, there is always light at the end of the tunnel and that light is You.

Amen.

December 4

BELIEVE IN JESUS

For it is by grace you have been saved, through faith –
and this not from yourselves, it is the gift of God.

EPHESIANS 2:8

*T*here is only one way that people can be saved: by believing in Jesus. We cannot bring about our own salvation, no matter what we do or how hard we try. It is a gift that comes to us from God alone. And He gives it to us because of His grace. All that we need to do is to receive His gift with thankful hearts.

You cannot satisfy God's requirements through what you do, and neither can you do anything to earn your salvation. But you can satisfy Him by believing in Jesus.

Thank You, Father, for Your wonderful gift of salvation.

Amen.

HE WILL MAKE YOU WELL

*"I have heard your prayer and seen your tears;
I will heal you. On the third day from now
you will go up to the temple of the LORD."*

2 KINGS 20:5

When King Hezekiah became terminally ill, he prayed that God would heal him. And God answered Hezekiah's prayer. He promised to heal him, and said that he would be able to go to the temple on the third day.

When you deal with sickness in your life you can be sure that God will hear your prayer and heal you, if that is His will. And even if you do not get well, you can bear testimony to Him from your sickbed.

Great Physician, if it is Your will, please heal those on their sickbeds. If it is not, please comfort them and their families.

Amen.

GOD IS AWARE OF YOUR HEARTACHE

Record my lament; list my tears on your scroll – are they not in your record?

PSALM 56:8

*T*he psalmist experienced times of great heartache. In these times he was comforted when he remembered that God knew about his anguish and that He saw each tear the psalmist cried. Each one was recorded in God's Book. God is never unmoved when His children's hearts are breaking.

God is aware of your heartache – each tear of yours is recorded in His Book! He really cares for you. And He eases the heartache of each one of His children.

Father, You see every tear that I cry. You feel my pain. Please comfort me and be with me. Amen.

WISDOM AND TACT

Peacemakers who sow in peace
raise a harvest of righteousness.

JAMES 3:18

*J*ames writes that anyone who needs wisdom can confidently ask God for it. He is prepared to give His wisdom to anyone who asks Him for it (see Jas. 1:5-6).

His wisdom teaches us to live differently from the way we lived before, and to enter into a right relationship with God and to live in peace with our neighbors.

To be a peacemaker in this world requires tact and wisdom – the kind of wisdom that only God can give you. Ask Him for it.

Lord, give me the wisdom to know right from wrong, and to sow peace where there is hatred. Amen.

IN HEAVEN

"There will be no more death or mourning or crying or pain, for the old order of things has passed away."

REVELATION 21:4

When John was given a revelation of God's new world, he discovered that things in heaven will be very different from the world that we know. No one will die there. Sorrow and suffering and pain will be things of the past. The children of God will be happy with God forever.

In hard times you can think about the eternal glory that God has promised to give you. With God in heaven there will be an end to all anguish, unhappiness and pain.

For now in this temporal life, remember that trials are only temporary.

Father, I know that I will not be sad or angry or unhappy forever. Trials are momentary. Your glory is forever and Your promise of eternal life true. Amen.

GOD GIVES JOY
AFTER THE SORROW

Those who sow in tears will reap with songs of joy.
He who goes out weeping, carrying seed to sow, will
return with songs of joy, carrying sheaves with him.

PSALM 126:5-6

God promises His children joy after sorrow. After the heartache of the exile, God's people could return to their own land with joy because God made a way for them. The people who sow in tears can, in faith, look forward to the day when they will reap the harvest in joy.

God can change your circumstances. He always turns sorrow into joy. He wants to turn your heartache into an abundant harvest today.

Lord, I give my circumstances to You, because I know that You can change them. Amen.

TALK TO HIM IN PRAYER

Train yourself to be godly.

1 TIMOTHY 4:7

Christians need to practice how to serve God, just as an athlete practices to stay fit.

If we really want to live a life committed to God, it will require sacrifice and practice on our part. And this kind of practice is much more important than physical exercise because it prepares you for heaven.

If you wish to be spiritually fit, you need to make time for Jesus Christ. Study your Bible regularly and talk to Him in prayer.

Father, I meditate on Your Word every day and look forward to every moment I can spend with You in prayer. Amen.

HE WALKS WITH YOU

For a man's ways are in full view of the
Lord, and he examines all his paths.

PROVERBS 5:21

*G*od knows everything there is to know about His children. Their lives are an open book before Him. He even sees each step they take.

Because God loves you, He walks with you each step of the way through life. Not only does He accompany you, but He examines each one of your steps! God knows all that you do and say, and knows exactly what you need.

He gives you strength to victoriously overcome each challenge that comes your way.

Every step I take, God, is known to You. And You are the one who keeps my foot from slipping. Amen.

LIFE IS A RACE

*Let us run with perseverance the race marked
out for us. Let us fix our eyes on Jesus,
the author and perfecter of our faith.*

HEBREWS 12:1-2

*T*he children of God have a head start in the race of life.
They know the secret of how to look away from the ob-
stacles in their way and to look to God. And they know
He will help them to the end of the course, and they will
end the race as victors if they trust in Him.

Your life here on earth is a race. Only if you keep your
eyes on Jesus will you have the spiritual strength that will
keep you in the race till the end.

*Father, I am running this race with my eyes firmly fixed on
You. Please help me to persevere to the very end.* *Amen.*

GOD LOOKS AFTER HIS CHILDREN

Praise awaits you, O God, in Zion; to you our vows will be fulfilled. You crown the year with your bounty, and your carts overflow with abundance.

PSALM 65:1, 11

The psalmist sings a praise song to God as the harvest is gathered in. He remembers that it is God who sends the rain that causes the grain to grow so that the animals will have sufficient food. It is God who makes the harvest grow and crowns the year with His gifts. Wherever He goes, He gives in abundance.

Just as God cares for creation around you, He also cares for each one of His children. When your life lines up with His will then it will become a song of praise.

Heavenly Father, wherever You go, You give in abundance. You take care of Your children so that they have all that they need. Amen.

GOD PROTECTS YOU

The angel of the LORD encamps around those who fear him, and he delivers them.

PSALM 34:7

We read many accounts in the Old Testament of how God protected His children and rescued them from danger. When they were in distress, He was always there to help them.

God is still able to protect His children. God knows about every distressing situation in your life. In such times He erects a hedge round about you to protect you. Ask for His help when you need Him, and He will give it to you.

Lord, I call out to You in my distress. I know that You will protect me. I will be safe in the shelter of Your wings. Amen.

December 15

THE HOLY SPIRIT
DEFENDS YOU

In the same way, the Spirit helps us in our weakness.
We do not know what we ought to pray for,
but the Spirit himself intercedes for us with
groans that words cannot express.

ROMANS 8:26

God gives His Holy Spirit to each of His children to teach us the right way to communicate with Him. When we don't know how to pray, when we cannot find the right words to offer in our petitions, then the Holy Spirit presents our case for us. He carries our requests directly to the throne room of God.

Just as an advocate defends a criminal in court, when you sin, the Holy Spirit defends your position before God.

Thank You, Lord Jesus, for sending us Your Holy Spirit to guide us and to offer up our petitions when we don't know what to pray. Amen.

MAKE YOURSELF AVAILABLE TO HIM

"I am the Lord's servant," Mary answered.
"May it be to me as you have said."

LUKE 1:38

Even though the angel brought a seemingly impossible message to Mary – that she would give birth to a Son even though she was a virgin – she was immediately prepared to make herself available for God to use. She did not give a thought to the problems that she would experience. She was prepared to obey God at once.

God can turn your problems into blessings if you are prepared to make yourself available to Him. If you are willing to do this, He will solve your problems.

Father, only You can turn my problems into wonderful blessings. That is why I give them all to You. Guide me into what it is You want me to do. Amen.

NO PLACE FOR JESUS

*She gave birth to her firstborn, a son. She wrapped
him in cloths and placed him in a manger,
because there was no room for them in the inn.*

LUKE 2:7

Bethlehem was crowded because of the census. Joseph and Mary were not able to find place at the inn and so the Son of God was born in a dirty stable. It was there that Mary gave birth to Him, wrapped Him in cloths and made Him a crib in the animal's feeding trough.

When Jesus was born, there was no room for Him at the inn. And today there are still many people who make no room for Him in their hearts and lives.

Invite Him into your heart again today.

Lord Jesus, I will make sure that there is always room for You in my heart and my life. As long as I live, I want You in my life. Amen.

December 18

GOOD NEWS

*When they had seen him, they spread
the word concerning what had been
told them about this child.*

LUKE 2:17

*T*he wonderful news the angels brought – that the long awaited Savior had been born in Bethlehem – was joyfully received by the shepherds. After the angels departed, they left everything just as it was and hurried to Bethlehem where they found Joseph, Mary and baby Jesus in a stable. They told them everything the angels had said about the Child.

When they left, they told the good news of the Savior's birth to everyone they saw. Do you tell others about the good news that you have heard?

Jesus Christ, You are my Savior and the Lord of my life. Please give me the courage and the wisdom to share the good news of Your salvation with everyone I meet. Amen.

A CHILD OF GOD

For you know the grace of our Lord Jesus Christ, that though he was rich, yet for your sakes he became poor, so that you through his poverty might become rich.

2 CORINTHIANS 8:9

*J*esus is so good to us – good beyond our understanding. He put aside the honor and glory that were His due for the sake of sinful people. He was prepared to come into the world as an ordinary person, so that all those who believe in Him can inherit the riches of heaven.

Jesus, the great King of all kings, was prepared to leave heaven and suffer the indignity of being born as a human baby so that you could become a child of God.

Thank God for His grace.

King above all kings, thank You for sacrificing the honor and the glory You deserved to be born into a sinful world, to die a horrible death and to be raised from the dead just so that I can be Your child. Amen.

WITHOUT FEAR

But the angel said to them, "Do not be afraid.
I bring you good news of great joy that will be for
all the people. Today in the town of David a Savior
has been born to you; he is Christ the Lord."

LUKE 2:10-11

The shepherds were initially terrified when they first saw the angel. But the angel calmed their fears. He told them that they had nothing to fear because the message that he brought was one of great joy: the Savior who had been expected for so long had been born at last.

Christians can live without fear. You need no longer be afraid of anything because your Savior was born two thousand years ago in Bethlehem.

Lord, my Savior and strength, You endured so much pain and
suffering on my behalf. I thank You, Lord and I praise You. All
glory belongs to You. Amen.

HE IS WITH YOU
EVERY DAY

"Fear not, for I have redeemed you;
I have summoned you by name; you are mine."

ISAIAH 43:1

Isaiah had a message of joy for the children of God: they could confidently unpack their burdens at His feet and leave them there and walk unimpeded through life. The God whom they worshiped set them free. He called them by name. They are His, both now and forever.

And this wonderful Redeemer is with you each day too. He lives in you through His Holy Spirit, and He protects and helps you.

Lord God, I lay my burdens at Your feet, because You set me free. Amen.

ALWAYS WITH YOU

"The virgin will be with child and will give birth to a son, and they will call him Immanuel" – which means, "God with us."

MATTHEW 1:23

The prophet Isaiah declared that God would give a sign to His people: a virgin would one day give birth to a Son. And the child would be called Immanuel, which means God is with us. He was the One who would set His people free from their sins (see Is. 7:14).

This prophecy came to pass on the first Christmas. Jesus was born of a virgin. And through His birth, God wants to let you know that He is always with you.

Omnipresent Father, Your goodness and mercy follow me all the days of my life. I need never be afraid, because You are always with me. Amen.

December 23

THE LIGHT
CONQUERS ETERNALLY

*The true light that gives light to every man
was coming into the world. ... The Word became
flesh and made his dwelling among us. We have
seen his glory, the glory of the One and Only,
who came from the Father, full of grace and truth.*

JOHN 1:9, 14

Isaiah also prophesied that the people who lived in darkness would see a great light (see Is. 7:1). John explained that Jesus, who is the true light of God, came into this world.

Jesus is the Word of God who became flesh and lived among us. He came to shine a light in our world darkened by sin. When He was born, the light overcame the darkness once and for all.

Father, we live in a dark, sin-filled world, but Your light drives out that darkness and renews our hope. Amen.

December 24

JESUS EXISTED FROM THE BEGINNING

*That which was from the beginning, which
we have heard, which we have seen with our eyes,
which we have looked at and our hands have
touched – this we proclaim concerning the Word of life.*

1 JOHN 1:1

Jesus was not just an ordinary person. He is God Himself. He has always existed. And yet ordinary people could hear Him speak, they could see Him and could even touch Him with their hands.

Jesus came to make it possible for people to approach God openly. Before He came to earth, no one could see God and live. Jesus has always existed. He is the Word and the Life. He came to earth to make a way for you to live with God forever.

Lord Jesus, You offered up Your own life to build a bridge between us and God. I praise You for Your sacrifice, mercy and forgiveness. Amen.

THE GREATEST GIFT
THE WORLD WILL EVER KNOW

Thanks be to God for his indescribable gift!

2 CORINTHIANS 9:15

*J*esus is the most wonderful gift of all time. Because God gave Him to the world on that first Christmas, He, through His death on the cross, made it possible for anyone who believes in Him to become children of God. We should never stop thanking God for Him.

When you and those you love give Christmas gifts to each other, you should not forget to thank God for Jesus Christ – He is the most wonderful gift that anyone could ever receive.

Heavenly Father, thank You for sacrificing Your only Son to save a sinful world. You gave us the most amazing gift anyone has ever known when You sent Jesus to save us. Amen.

PATHS OF PEACE

*... Because of the tender mercy of our God, by which
the rising sun will come to us from heaven to shine on
those living in darkness and in the shadow of death,
to guide our feet into the path of peace.*

LUKE 1:78-79

*T*he prophet Zechariah prophesied that the Child that
was to be born would be like the morning sun. He would
cause the grace of God to shine in all the world and bring
light to the people who still lived in the shadow and
darkness of death. He would make it possible for them
to follow the path of peace.

Only Christ can give you true and lasting peace. Only
He can help you walk in paths of peace.

*Prince of Peace, You are the bright Light who came to drive
the darkness from our lives. Because of You, we can still have
hope in the darkest of times. Amen.*

December 27

HIS GOODNESS IS YOURS

*For his anger lasts only a moment, but his favor
lasts a lifetime; weeping may remain for a night,
but rejoicing comes in the morning.*

PSALM 30:5

*G*od does not stay angry for long, but His faithful love
for His children lasts forever. Jesus earned forgiveness for
us when He died on the cross, and so God is no longer
angry with us because of our sins. But this does not guarantee that His children will be free from difficulties.

When dark times come into your life, you can trust
in God. He is always there to help you and to solve your
problems for you. His anger lasts for a moment, but His
goodness is with you your whole life long.

*Father, all of my problems and fears and worries I bring to
You. Be gracious to me and help me.* Amen.

December 28

ACCORDING TO GOD'S WILL

"Therefore I tell you, whatever you ask for in prayer, believe that you have received it, and it will be yours."

MARK 11:24

*J*esus assured His disciples that when people pray and believe, they will receive what they ask of God. And yet there is a single condition attached to this promise: God does not answer prayers that are not in accordance with His will.

When you pray according to God's will, you can be so sure that He will answer you. You can thank Him even before you see the answer to your prayer.

Father God, let Your will be done in my life. Amen.

LOOK PAST
THE PROBLEMS

I believed; therefore I said, "I am greatly afflicted."

PSALM 116:10

*O*ver and again the psalmist experienced God's deliverance when his life was in danger. In these challenging times, he could still keep believing in God, even when he thought there was no way out.

Trust and faith still work in the midst of crises. Even though your troubles might sometimes seem insurmountable, you can look past them and see God; you can keep believing in Him even when you think there's no hope. God is there when you have nothing at all.

Heavenly Father, Your faithfulness knows no end. Even when I face insurmountable challenges, I can rest assured that You will keep Your promise of love and protection. Amen.

IN THE FUTURE

*But you will not leave in haste or go in flight;
for the LORD will go before you, the God
of Israel will be your rear guard.*

ISAIAH 52:12

God assured His people that they did not need to flee in haste from Babylon. He promises to go ahead of them to lead them and to protect them from behind.

Just as God has walked with you through the year that has passed, He wants to be with you each day of the future. He wants to walk ahead of you into the new year. He will go before you to show you the way, and He will be behind you to keep you safe.

Heavenly Father, I can confidently go into each day, knowing that You will protect me and guide me. No matter what happens, You will be there to help me. Amen.

December 31

THE RIGHT ROAD

*Whether you turn to the right or to the left,
your ears will hear a voice behind you,
saying, "This is the way; walk in it."*

ISAIAH 30:21

We all sometimes lose our way and take a detour from God's path. If this should happen to you, God promises that you will hear a voice behind you that will direct you on the right path.

In the year that has passed, you experienced God with you each day. And He wants to lead you into the new year. Make sure that you are sensitive to His voice.

You are surrounded by and filled with God's love. As the new year approaches, make a resolution to share His infinite love with everyone in your life.

*When I stray from the right path, Lord, guide me back to You.
Lead me where I should go. Amen.*

Faith makes
the impossible
possible!